MILITARY LIFE 101

MILITARY 101

Basic Training for
New Military Families

JANET I. FARLEY

ROWMAN & LITTLEFIELD
Lanham • Boulder • New York • London

Published by Rowman & Littlefield
A wholly owned subsidiary of The Rowman & Littlefield Publishing Group, Inc.
4501 Forbes Boulevard, Suite 200, Lanham, Maryland 20706
www.rowman.com

Unit A, Whitacre Mews, 26-34 Stannary Street, London SE11 4AB

British Library Cataloguing in Publication Information Available

Library of Congress Cataloging-in-Publication Data

Names: Farley, Janet I., author.
Title: Military life 101 : basic training for new military families / Janet I. Farley.
Other titles: Basic training for new military families
Description: Lanham : Rowan & Littlefield, [2016] | Includes bibliographical
   references and index.
Identifiers: LCCN 2015050849 (print) | LCCN 2016000179 (ebook) | ISBN
   9781442256019 (cloth : alk. paper) | ISBN 9781442256026 (electronic) |
   ISBN 9781442256026 (Electronic)
Subjects: LCSH: Military spouses—United States—Handbooks, manuals, etc. |
   Families of military personnel—United States—Handbooks, manuals, etc. |
   United States—Armed Forces—Military life—Handbooks, manuals, etc.
Classification: LCC U766 .F37 2016 (print) | LCC U766 (ebook) | DDC
   355.1/20973—dc23
LC record available at http://lccn.loc.gov/2015050849

∞™ The paper used in this publication meets the minimum requirements of
American National Standard for Information Sciences—Permanence of Paper
for Printed Library Materials, ANSI/NISO Z39.48-1992.

Printed in the United States of America

DEDICATION

This book is dedicated to U.S. service members of the past, present, and future; their family members who love them; and the many committed service providers who work faithfully in and around the Department of Defense in support of them.

Semper Fi.
Hooah.

CONTENTS

ACKNOWLEDGMENTS

When Kathryn Knigge of Rowman & Littlefield Publishers contacted me and invited me to submit a proposal about military life for their expanding collection of related titles, I was elated. I am thankful to her for the interest in our military families and for her willingness to work with me on this project. I also appreciate the hard work of all those who helped to bring this book to publication at Rowman & Littlefield.

A debt of gratitude is owed to many, and I will try to mention those names here and hope that I do not miss anyone because the efforts of all have been so important in the creation of this book. If I did miss someone, please forgive me.

If you want to know how military families succeed in this ever-changing world, you ask military families. They are the true experts. Their much-appreciated and more-than-generous wisdom is included throughout the pages of this book. Thank you on that note to Terri Barnes, Nat Benipayo, Rebecca Bring, Carmen Carlisle, Stephanie Hodges, Karen Jamison, Emily Jamison, Nick Johnson, Aubrey Kaufman, Tanya Kerr, Karen Kramp, Pam Cabana Macken, Debbie Milby, Shavonne Black-Moore, Jessica Leia Moss, Kaylin Neiheisel, Kate Numerick, Sonia Greer, Robert Greer, Jennifer Oswalt, Rebecca Roth, Hannah Schlagel, Kristin Sells, Siggi, Heather Smith, Heather Unruh, and Denise Wright.

My thanks also to the military family members who contributed their wisdom but who wished to remain anonymous.

I've always believed that you don't have to know everything if you know the right expert to call upon who is willing to share his or her knowledge with you.

With that concept in mind, thanks to Arcelio Arylene, a financial readiness program specialist, for his kind assistance in the development of chapter 2, "Military Money and Benefits." The ever-charismatic Mr. Arylene works tirelessly in support of the financial health and well-being of military service members and families across the services.

I would to thank two of my favorite high school seniors, Frannie Farley and Erzsebet Kalwaitis (Class of 2016) for their online research abilities and for knocking out volunteer hours at the same time. You go, girls.

If you're lucky, the best friends you meet because of the military become more like members of your own family through the years. They also encourage you when you write your book. Thanks to Donna Daniels and Chris Hamilton, my sisters by choice, who supported and drank with me even as they each launched their own worldwide PCS moves in the process.

Sometimes people you have worked with and respect from afar say just the right thing when you most need to hear it. Kerry McGinley knows what I'm talking about, and I hope she knows I appreciate her for it. I also appreciate the kind words of Kristyne Torruella, who said, "It's going to be a great book, Janet," on a Facebook thread. I printed that out and looked at it every day. I like to believe she was right.

Thank you to Farley, the best husband in the world, who has been so incredibly supportive through my very long hours spent writing this book. And thank you to my two amazingly beautiful daughters, Frannie and Terrie, and our furball, Bella. Your love, support, and humorous daily antics make my life a truly rich one. I wouldn't want things any other way. Now stop growing up so fast. I like having you around.

For twenty-plus years, I have made it my professional mission to make a positive difference in the lives of our military service and family members. I have tried to do that by serving in positions, both paid and volunteer, that afforded me the opportunity to make a difference. I have worked as a career counselor, an employment program manager, a military spouse career and education program analyst, a transition assistance program manager, and as a military family and careers columnist who has wanted to increase awareness about issues that matter to all of us through the written word.

I hope that has happened here.

INTRODUCTION

Before I started writing *Military Life 101: Basic Training for New Military Families*, I ran into Karen, an old friend of mine on the military post I call my own. Our chance encounter influenced this book in what I like to think is a positive way.

Let me explain.

Karen and I have known each other for years. Both she and her husband are retired Naval officers who now work for the federal government. We met through our husbands, who served together in a joint military command in Germany while on active duty.

Coincidentally, her sailor and my soldier worked together again in life after the uniform, too. If you stick around the military long enough, you'll see that kind of thing happens frequently in a big world that can seem incredibly small at times.

Karen had happy news to share with me that day. Somehow, in the blink of an eye, her military brat grew up, joined the Navy, fell in love, and married a young lady named Emily, all in that order.

Emily was, of course, smitten with her dashing young sailor. What's not to like about a handsome guy in a military uniform, right? The unfamiliar military lifestyle she suddenly found herself living, on the other hand, left her thoroughly confused and bewildered.

Things might not have been clear for Emily, but they were starting to become clear for me. It was at that very moment that this book started coming together nicely in my headspace.

CONFUSION AND BEWILDERMENT ALL AROUND

After that chance meeting with my friend, I thought quite a bit about Emily, and something else occurred to me in the process.

Spouses and family members new to this lifestyle, it would seem, aren't the only ones who are confused and bewildered about military life.

If not-so-distant headlines are to be believed, many other Americans are slightly confused and bewildered as well.

According to one article in the *New York Times*, "The greatest challenge to our military is not from a foreign enemy—it's the widening gap between the American people and their armed forces."[1]

That gap shouldn't come as too much of a surprise to us, however, given the small number of people who actually wear the military uniform. Less than one-half of 1 percent of our citizens serves our country in uniform.[2]

Unless you are a part of a multigenerational military family or live and work familiarly within a military community, you might not understand what it is that they do and what kind of life exists behind the front gate of a military installation.

Or worse, you might think you understand it, but you could be misunderstanding it altogether. Military life can be confusing at times for those who live in the world. Imagine how confusing it must be for those who aren't around it at all.

"During the war years, we all were so focused on just getting through one deployment after another that we felt we didn't have the time to explain our challenges to the civilian world. Maybe we didn't. We were hunkered down, just getting through the best way we could," said Terri Barnes, my good friend, award-winning columnist and author of *Spouse Calls: Messages from a Military Life* (2014).

She thinks we are living with the consequences now.

"Civilians, exposed mostly to homecoming videos and stories about PTSD, don't have a true picture of the life we live, the challenges we face and they might not even understand the function of a military during more peaceful times," she said.

"It's more important now than ever that we communicate with people outside the front gate to emphasize that we are not just a subculture. We are an integral part of American society. The nation needs its military, and we need our nation," she said. The military-to-civilian disconnect might not ever fully dissolve, but we can each do our own part, big or small, to minimize the greater misunderstandings and facilitate a mutual appreciation.

Terri offers us these tips, and they are good ones for all of us to know whether we are new to the military or not:

- Listen to your civilian neighbors.
- Share your own stories with those outside of the military.
- Build individual and family relationships in your communities.

"We don't need a public relations campaign. We need real people connecting with real people across the military-civilian divide," she said.

I couldn't agree with her more.

Relationship building is key to understanding. We don't all have to agree on our life choices, our politics, or our beliefs. We are, however, the *United* States, and that would suggest in my mind that we should at least strive to have a good understanding and appreciation of one other.

The diversity within our country is what makes us unique in the first place. It's what will keep us strong moving forward if we keep our minds and hearts open to our differences.

New military family members, such as you, are going to be instrumental in making that military and civilian divide fade away over time.

You, after all, are in a unique position to make those connections with others both across the apparent divide and within the greater military family itself.

You might be able to better explain military life to others, however, after you understand it a little better yourself.

WHO THIS BOOK IS WRITTEN FOR

Military Life 101: Basic Training for New Military Families was written for young Emily and those like her who find themselves living in a strange, new world.

It is my sincere hope that this book does a great job of answering the simple question: "What would Emily (and other new military spouses) need to know to get by here?"

Military Life 101: Basic Training for New Military Families is also written for:

- those considering a career in uniform and wondering how that decision could potentially impact family members
- service providers who work or volunteer within a military community and desire a greater understanding of it

- military leaders, family readiness group members, ombudsmen, or key spouses who may be looking for training resources to help introduce new families to the military lifestyle
- anyone seeking to narrow the widening gap between the military and civilian communities

AN OVERVIEW OF COMING ATTRACTIONS

Military Life 101: Basic Training for New Military Families painlessly provides new families or those considering a career in uniform the culturally relevant and need-to-know *now* information required to survive and thrive in this ever-evolving lifestyle.

The book is flexible in sequence and may easily be read cover to cover or not. If you've just received orders to move, jump to chapter 4, "Mastering Military Moves," immediately! You can catch up on the rest as you need it.

Here is what you'll find in the book when you do:

In chapter 1, "Great Expectations," you'll get an overview of your new normal. You'll learn about the all-important first steps that must be taken as you land "boots on the ground" in this world.

It won't take you long to figure out that the military has a vocabulary of its very own, and we'll address that in this chapter. You'll even learn how to tell time, military style.

You may not wear the military uniform, but it certainly doesn't hurt to know a little something about the different military ranks, pay grades, and insignia. You'll get a brief overview of those here as well.

Finally, you'll become acquainted with some of the common, time-honored military customs and courtesies observed in all branches of service.

Chapter 2, "Military Money and Benefits," clearly explains the basics of military pay and allowances. We'll decipher the leave and earnings statement (LES) for you and show you how to effectively manage your money so you won't have to live paycheck to paycheck, which is always a good thing, right?

You'll also learn about important family benefits, and we'll discuss the importance of having good credit in the military.

Finally, we'll show you how to spot a financial scam and explain how to protect yourself from the growing problem of identity theft.

In chapter 3, "Military Family Support," you'll be introduced to many of the important installation resources you will come to rely on throughout your tenure as a military family, including the programs and services of the family support centers and the Morale, Welfare and Recreation (MWR) programs.

In this chapter, you'll learn about the cost-savings shopping options typically found on most military installations and about military-run lodging facilities where you can stay until you are assigned government housing or until you find a place to live within the local community.

If you ever find yourself stationed overseas, you'll be pleased to learn about the first-class entertainment provided to you by the Armed Forces Entertainment branch of the Department of Defense (DoD).

You'll also learn about the Armed Forces Recreation Center and the exciting vacation planning options that may be open to you throughout the world at affordable rates.

In this chapter, you'll also be introduced to some of the big-name, nonprofit organizations and other similar service-related resources that partner with the DoD and do many good things in support of military families.

Chances are fairly high that you will move once or twice while you are a part of a military family. It's never an easy task, but there are things you can do to make the process less painful for all involved. In chapter 4, "Mastering Military Moves," you'll learn how to effectively navigate a Permanent Change of Station (PCS) move like someone who has done it time and time again.

You'll learn how to coordinate your relocation through the transportation office and become familiar with typical moving allowances that may be available to your family, depending on your service member's circumstances.

You'll get the lowdown on how to successfully prepare and execute a major household move, before, during, and after the moving truck arrives.

If you have orders moving your family overseas, you'll soon find that it's different from moving within the United States. The tips provided in this chapter can help you and your family to adjust more quickly to life abroad.

Finally, not all moves involve the whole family. Sometimes your uniformed loved one packs his bags for a tour of duty without you. In this chapter, we also discuss the unaccompanied move and give you a few good strategies to help you and your family deal with it.

If you are a professionally minded military spouse, you may find yourself having some unique employment challenges, too. In chapter 5, "Military Spouse Careers and Education," we'll discuss those challenges so you can at least be aware of them. We'll also go over the basics you need to know to find a good job and progress your career wherever you happen to be stationed.

If you are considering a job in the federal government or have an interest in starting your own business, then you'll appreciate the many tried-and-true tips you will find here. Included in this section are must-know tips for creating an account and navigating the USAJobs website.

Some of the hardest times a family experiences in the military happen when service members are called to serve elsewhere, leaving you and your family behind to wait, worry, and adapt to a life without the one you love until his or her return.

In chapter 6, "Dealing with Deployments and Other Separations," you'll learn how you and your children can survive and thrive whenever your spouse deploys or otherwise has to leave you for the job for an extended period of time.

The military lifestyle is a unique one, full of many, at times, heavy stressors. In chapter 7, "Difficult Topics in Military Life," we discuss a few topics that no one likes to talk about in any world. Nevertheless, we do so here because they are also a potential part of military life. For example, we'll address the relatively recent rise of online haters within the military community itself.

Because military life is full of stressors, we'll provide you with the information you need to know to recognize and deal with stress in yourself and others. We'll also broach some other hard subjects such as suicide, domestic abuse, sexual assault, and divorce.

Those who serve in the military don't exactly work nine-to-five jobs. When the job takes service members to serve stress harm's way, bad things can, and sadly, do happen. This chapter will tell you about the important resources you should know about in case those events happen to you or someone you know.

Finally, in chapter 8, "Mission Transition," we oddly fast-forward to the end of your uniformed spouse's tour in the military, and for good reason. There are actions that you both can proactively take now at this stage of your journey that will benefit your family when the time comes to transition out of the military lifestyle, whether that is two years from now or twenty years plus from now.

In the appendixes, you'll find useful resources. First, you'll find a *Military Life 101* Recommended Reading List. I'm a firm believer in books and getting smart on topics that can help you do good things. In Appendix B, you'll find a list of commonly used military terms and expressions and their English translations to help you decipher some of the strange, new words you may wonder about.

Many of the fabulous books on the recommended reading list are written by authors I professionally and/or personally know who call the military community their own. They are very smart people who have made positive differences in the lives of many, and they are excellent role models for all of us. They offer a wealth of knowledge, experience, comfort, and counsel to you.

There's a little something else for you to savor in *Military Life 101: Basic Training for New Military Families*, too.

Sprinkled throughout this book, like just the right amount of seasoning, you'll find sound bites of good advice offered up freely by fellow military family members from around the world. Some of the best advice you'll ever receive is from fellow spouses and service members who have learned the hard way what works and what doesn't.

WHAT THIS BOOK WON'T DO FOR YOU

This book won't provide you with the answers to all of your questions. It wasn't designed to do so in the first place. It is meant to give you just enough information to get you up to speed on the basics you need to know now in a friendly, honest, and direct way.

Of course, you're going to have a lot of questions. Many of them will be answered here. Armed with the information provided in this book, you'll know where to go to find those answers for the ones that aren't.

A LITTLE SOMETHING ABOUT THE AUTHOR

Military Life 101: Basic Training for New Military Families is written by someone who is a U.S. Marine Corps brat, an Army wife, and a career consultant with over twenty-two years of military to civilian and military spouse employment expertise. I have also worked and volunteered extensively within military family support centers where I was privileged to meet new military family members and help them feel at home in the military lifestyle.

I care deeply about the greater military family, as it is truly my own family. You are now a part of that family or are soon to be, so I care about you, too. It is my sincerest hope that this book serves you well in this new chapter of your life.

While I know quite a bit about many aspects of military life, I certainly don't know everything. This book, fortunately for all of us, includes volunteered expertise and insight from multiple expert sources. I have hopefully given credit where it is deserved in the acknowledgments section of this book.

OF VIEWPOINTS, SEMANTICS, AND ASSUMPTIONS

Military Life 101: Basic Training for New Military Families is written for military family members, but perhaps more specifically with military spouses in mind.

As you read this book, it may appear that gender and family dynamic assumptions are being made. I'd like to explain myself now before anyone takes unnecessary offense.

Throughout much of the book, I refer to service members primarily as male and military spouses as female. Of course, service members can be and are either outside the pages of this book. I didn't think you would like to continually read expressions like *his or her, he or she,* and I didn't want to continue awkwardly using those expressions either.

It may also appear that the typical military family is assumed to be made up of a military spouse, a uniformed service member, and a couple of kids thrown in for good measure. No offense is intended here to dual-serving military families, single parents, families that have no children, or single service members.

Military service members and military families are wonderfully diverse. That diversity is in fact one of the greatest things about military life, and I am well aware of it. You should be, too.

The writing conventions used inside the pages of this book, however, were done in this manner so that reading the content would flow easier for you and writing it easier for me.

I truly hope you enjoy this book, and I hope it helps you feel more at home in the military lifestyle. If you like to share your thoughts on it or your ideas for future revisions, please contact me at through Rowman & Littlefield.

1

GREAT EXPECTATIONS

Being [in the] military is a sacrifice for everyone, not just the service member, so it's like the entire family has signed on that dotted line.

—Jessica Leia Moss, U.S. Coast Guard Brat and U.S. Air Force Spouse

Welcome to the greater military family, newbie! It doesn't matter whether you are a part of an Army, Air Force, Navy, Marine Corps, or Coast Guard family. You're in for quite an adventure. Even if you already know about military life, perhaps you even served in uniform yourself, things always look and feel a little bit different from the spousal perspective.

Living la vida military is definitely a unique experience, and not one that everyone is cut out to lead. Without a doubt, the one who wears the uniform has a tough and often unpredictable job that doesn't fit neatly into a typical nine-to-five workday category.

Being married to someone who wears the uniform can be a tough job, too. You may not have signed on the dotted line to serve our country, but you do it anyway. Your life and the lives of any children you happen to have is directly impacted by your spouse's career choice, nevertheless.

I was an Air Force brat, and I was in the Army National Guard. I had some knowledge of military life when I married my husband, who joined the Army six months after we were married. Even though I knew some things about the military life, it is much different being a military spouse.

—Rebecca Roth, U.S. Army Spouse

The truth is that sometimes that impact is positive, and sometimes it's not.

HOLLYWOOD VERSUS REAL LIFE

So what, exactly, can someone who's new to military life expect of it?

Good question. *Complicated answer.*

Here's the thing. The military community itself is made up of many different people. As a result, how one experiences it may differ significantly from how someone else does, making an easy answer basically nonexistent.

On the big screen, Hollywood has tried to answer the question, at least in part, for the inquiring minds among us.

Through blockbuster movies such as *American Sniper, The Hurt Locker,* and others, Hollywood has attempted to depict what it's like to serve in uniform today, and they've done a fabulous job of building exciting story lines, based in reality, around unique personas.

They have also attempted to capture the essence of military life and its effect on families, but they haven't fully succeeded in doing so save the requisite poignant glance a solemn spouse gives her uniformed hunk as he heads off to war.

Many living in the military life itself might agree it has been a hit and miss on the family note. Perhaps reality would result in much lower box office numbers.

Instead, those unfamiliar with the military believe what they see on the big screen, and it can be misleading. Everyone who serves in uniform certainly knows how to do what he or she has to do in times of war. That is their job first and foremost, and they are the best at doing it.

Not everyone who serves in uniform, however, is a high-speed, low-drag special operations sniper or bomb expert. People serve in many other career occupations across the services, too. The military's special forces and infantry may get all the big-screen time, but service members also work in information technology, health care, logistics, engineering, intelligence, finance, music, and so much more. Any military recruiter will be happy to explain it to you. Variety, it's said, is the spice of life, and there is a lot of variety in all the service branches.

Within any military community, you will find people from all walks of life at different ages and stages of their own lives.

Let's back up a bit and take a brief look at some of the facts and figures.

- We are great in numbers. There are 2,204,839 military personnel (active and reserves) and 2,978,341 family members, including spouses, children, and adult dependents.[1]
- There are nearly three million military family members. Of those, over a million are spouses. Nearly half of them (46 percent) are thirty years of age or younger.[2] There are 1,076,564 military spouses, and over 65 percent of those spouses are thirty-five years old or younger, while 34.8 percent are thirty-six years of age or older. Most military spouses are women, but a growing number of men are spouses, too.
- There are 1,888,486 military children, with nearly 92.9 percent of those children aged birth to eighteen years old and 7.1 percent being nineteen to twenty-two years of age.
- On average, military families move because of the job every two to three years. This is ten times more than civilian families.
- We believe in what our spouses do for a living. A whopping 91 percent of those surveyed in the military community believe in the importance of service in the military or some other type of national service. While our political views may not always agree with marching orders, our hearts and minds are definitely with our uniformed loved ones.
- We are stressed out, and with good reasons. A growing trend featuring uncertainty about military life is all too real.[3] Military pay and retirement benefit changes, along with spouse employment, military suicide, and veteran employment are what we reportedly worry the most about. There are other things, too. Deployments or separations, frequent moves, and feelings of isolation from friends or family remain loyal stressors in our lives as well.[4]

I have [lived] in all stages of military life. I was a military child, on active duty myself, married to someone on active duty, on active duty with a retired military spouse, and a retired service member and "retired" spouse. I am now a civilian spouse. One thing I have learned is that not every stage [of the military lifestyle] is the same. I have to roll with the punches as they come. I have to enjoy each stage as its own adventure. I cannot compare stages because it would be comparing apples to oranges. Be prepared for anything since you don't know what is around the corner.

—Karen Kramp, U.S. Air Force Spouse (Retired)

Facts and figures speak to the big picture. Everyday realities, however, can be found behind the numbers.

We may live in a democracy, but it doesn't seem like our uniformed service members serve in one.

Instead, they willingly work in a world where someone tells someone else what to do and expects it to get done without asking questions. Everyone has a boss, and rank has its at least perceived privileges, to be sure.

It may sound like an unfair environment, and at times it certainly is. There's a good reason for this mentality, however. It works. It works particularly well when it needs to do so in order to save lives.

It may help you to remember that your spouse doesn't work in a typical nine-to-five job. As such, don't expect a typical lifestyle. You'll be terribly disappointed.

No matter how old you are or what rank your service member wears, you'll quickly find that military life is a life like no other.

Whether you call the uniformed family yours for a short tour or for a lifetime, you're sure to have some unique and memorable experiences along the way.

> I love every second of it. You get to have some great experiences and live in a world where everyone is willing to step up, help, and be there when you need it the most. You have to be able to adjust to it, though, and accept the line of duty for your spouse.
>
> —Kaylin Neiheisel, U.S. Army Spouse

There will be times you and your loved one are separated. You won't know where he or she is exactly, and you will wonder when you will get a phone call, a letter, or an email.

> There were days when I waited and wondered if or when my soldier would call and wondered why he did not. These were the times where my character was tested, and I realized how fallible I was as a human being.
>
> —Sonia Greer, U.S. Army Spouse

You can bet your spouse will miss countless dinners with your family at night, birthdays, anniversaries, and other important milestones.

There are times your spouse has to work late, do a weeklong field training exercise, go on TDY (travel to another place for short periods of time), or you get orders to move someplace you have never heard of. You learn quickly that you have no control.

—Rebecca Roth, U.S. Army Spouse

He or she may love you more than anyone in the world, but the military and its missions will take priority over you and your marriage more times than you'll even want to imagine at this point.

Warning. Emotions may run high.

There will be times when you are angry. You will not be overly fond of the military because of its uncontrollable influence over your life. You will wonder why you ever agreed to this career path, if you even did in the first place. Expect anger to appear on the day your spouse has a duffel bag or a suitcase packed and is about to kiss you goodbye.

Those days are not good days by any stretch of the imagination.

You may have no idea where he is actually going, when he will come home, or when you will hear from him again. Worry will become your trusted companion, and waiting for his safe return your new pastime—that is, when you have a rare moment to yourself.

Since he will be gone, you will be handling everything on the home front. If you're not already a jack of all trades, you will become one, as things will go wrong. *You can count on it.* The car will break down. The refrigerator will go out. There will be a natural disaster and broken bones somewhere between one unfortunate event and the next.

If you have children, they will experience more in their sweet, young lives than others experience in a whole lifetime, and that can be a real catch-22 at times.

You will wake up one day and realize that your brats (because that's what they are affectionately called in this world) are far more resilient than others their age.

Except when they're not. It's hard to be resilient when they have to say goodbye to their new best friends over and over again. Or when they have to take additional classes in order to graduate from high school because their credits weren't accepted between the last high school and the new one.

There will be times when you are professionally frustrated, too. It can be difficult to build a career when you move every two to three years. You may come to resent your situation quickly.

It would be wrong to tell you that your life in the military family will be an easy one or even a predictable one. It will, however, be a unique one. If you are capable of flexibility, adaptability, and humor, and you have a taste for adventure, then you'll be just fine.

While there are many challenges and hardships, there are many truly wonderful and exciting things, too.

You will experience life in new places. Military orders may send your family to some truly exciting locations such as Hawaii, Alaska, Europe, the Pacific, and Asia. Or not. You may get orders to places that aren't so exciting, populated, or even close to someplace that is. Either way, you will see new places and experience what life is like there.

Your family will grow. You may or may not have children, but you will develop genuine and lifelong friendships with people you may have never met without this military connection. They will become members of your extended family who you may even love more than some of your own distant family members. The inevitable years and miles apart won't affect the strength of those relationships. They will be solid.

You won't starve. The military perks are pretty good, and the paychecks are fairly regular. Knock on wood for good luck, but past government shutdowns or threats of them haven't prevented service members from receiving their paychecks on a bimonthly basis. There are also a whole slew of entitlements, special pays, and allowances that your service member might receive at some point or another during his time in uniform. To learn more about those, see chapter 2, "Military Money and Benefits."

> The running joke in my family is that my husband is married to Uncle Sam and that I am his mistress. Like anything, marriage is hard work. We do sacrifice a lot being a military spouse, but I feel what I have gained far outweighs the negative.
>
> —Rebecca Roth, U.S. Army Spouse

Life will be dynamic in nature. The unexpected often happens in military life. You can go ahead and safely assume uncertainty will be your new normal. You won't always know where you are moving next. You won't always know when you will hear from your deployed loved one. You won't always know how you are going to make ends meet.

When facing the uncertainty of military life, it is important to be cohesive and healthy as a couple and as a family. The stressors of military life can get to all of us. We may be far away from our normal support system and living in unfamiliar places. The important thing is to do preventative maintenance where you can and pull in outside help when it is needed.

—Jennifer Oswalt, U.S. Air Force Spouse

MILITARY FAMILIES MATTER

While you don't actively serve in the military, you are a big and important part of the military family. You are one-half of the command team in your family, and your role is important all the time even if you don't get a paycheck for it.

- It matters when you are first married and you don't know the difference between an LES and PX/BX. (Confused? Don't be. We'll discuss common acronyms soon.)
- It matters as your spouse rises through the ranks and you become the unofficial person that other new spouses may turn to when they're in trouble or when they need to better understand things.
- It matters as you transition out of the military when your common attentions turn to your civilian life together.

It may not always seem like it in your military life journey, but you and your family matter a great deal to the DoD.

Great efforts are made, even when budgets are tight, by those working at the upper levels of government to facilitate your overall satisfaction with military life.

You don't serve in uniform, so why does this matter to the DoD?

The logic is simple. Service members who have spouses, partners, and children who are satisfied with their lives tend to stay in uniform. Having a trained, experienced, and focused military force is crucial to mission success and readiness. When family members aren't happy, then service members don't stay in the military. They leave, and they take with them valuable skills and experience that will cost the DoD a whole bunch to eventually obtain in someone else.

I thought that life in the military would be the "perfect life." By perfect life, I mean no drama, free sailing, and my husband would return home by dinner every night, at least for the most part. I was completely wrong.

—Kaylin Neiheisel, U.S. Army Spouse

YOUR FAMILY'S MUST-TAKE FIRST STEPS

Take a drive on any U.S. military installation, and you'll see a world existing within a world regardless of the size of it.

Of course, before you can do that, first you have to get past the front gate guard, right? How do you do that? You do that with your official club card, of course.

It's called a military identification card, or simply an ID card for short. How do you get that? Easy. First, marry someone in the military.

Your service member (also called your sponsor) enrolls you and any eligible family members in the Defense Enrollment Eligibility Reporting System (DEERS) through his or her personnel office. Afterward, you are able to go to the Pass and ID office on the nearest military installation and get one. Your service member or sponsor will most likely have to go with you, too.

As a military spouse, you should be eligible to use all the services on the installation. Be sure your ID cards states that, too; otherwise, you might have issues later when you try to and notice that your card won't allow you access to some building or service.

Once you have your ID card, protect it. Keep it in your wallet in a safe place, and don't lose it. Bad guys would love to get their hands on it so they could have access to things they shouldn't get access to ever.

If you do happen to lose it, notify the military police immediately and get a new one issued to you. You're going to need it over and over again to do just about anything except breathe on a military installation. For example, you'll need it to:

- enter any guarded military post (what the Army calls it) or base (what every other branch of service calls it)
- shop at the commissary (the grocery store) or the exchange (department store)
- receive health care benefits
- go to the movie theater

- use the Morale, Welfare and Recreation (MWR) facilities (See chapter 3, "Military Family Support," for more information about MWR.)
- sign up for college classes at the military education center
- show the military policeman when you get stopped for driving too fast on the installation

If you have children, they are eligible to get an ID card when they are ten years old. Getting a first ID card is a rite of passage in the life of a military brat. Snap a photo while they smile for the mug shot. Embarrass them. It's what we do to mark the occasion of our little darlings who are growing way too fast.

Getting enrolled in DEERS is crucial. It confirms that you are a member of the military family in the eyes of the DoD. It is the proof to service providers that you are eligible for health care, special pay, and other benefits.

Information about you, your service member, and other eligible families in DEERS should be correct and current at all times.

For example, if you have a baby, you need to make sure the new addition in your life is added to DEERS. You won't be able to get his well-baby checkups at the military clinic if you don't. When that baby grows up to be his or her own adult, then DEERS has to be updated there, too.

You can't enroll yourself or make any changes to DEERS. Only the service member can, and it is his or her responsibility to do so. Supporting documentation may be necessary to make it happen, such as a copy of your marriage license, birth certificates, and Social Security cards of all family members.

Once you and any other family members are enrolled in DEERS, you can begin to take advantage of the many benefits available to you. You'll learn more about all these benefits throughout the basic training provided in this book.

Getting enrolled in DEERS is crucial, but it is certainly not the only important business you need to take care of as you enter la vida military.

Here are some other first steps to take as a new military family:

- Memorize your spouse's Social Security number. You'll need it far more than you will need your own. In fact, you might wonder why you even have one at some point, but I digress. Don't freely write it down where others can see it, however. For more information about protecting your identity (and your sponsor's), see chapter 2, "Military Money and Benefits."

- Get a power of attorney. At some point, your uniformed loved one will be gone when you need to take care of legal matters. He will be deployed, on temporary duty somewhere else (TDY/TAD), away at some school, or otherwise separated from you because of work and world issues. You may need to have this legal authority to take care of business matters sans obstacles. You can obtain a power of attorney free of charge at the military legal services office on your installation.
- Make sure your spouse has a designated beneficiary on the Servicemember Group Life Insurance (SGLI). As the love of his or her life, you should be that beneficiary. Active duty service members are automatically enrolled in SGLI, which provides low-cost term life insurance coverage. Learn more about SGLI at http://www.benefits.va.gov/insurance/sgli.asp and in chapter 2, "Military Money and Benefits."
- Make sure your spouse's next of kin and emergency data (DD Form 93) are updated. No one likes to think that bad things will ever happen. Sometimes, however, they do, particularly in this line of work. Incorrect or out-of-date information on this important legal document will only make things worse for those left behind.
- Get or update your wills. Again, you can do this free of charge (with your high-speed ID card, of course) at the military legal services office on your installation.
- Register your car(s) on the installation so you can drive it there. You'll need to bring your driver's license, vehicle registration, and proof of auto insurance. Depending on the installation, you will need to do this through the military police (MP) office, the Provost Marshall's Office (PMO) (the mother of all MPs), or a nondescript office aptly called something like the vehicle registration office. If you are registering your car on a stateside installation, you will probably be given a sticker for your car. Overseas, however, you will be required to ditch any sticker on your car that gives you away as an American, for security's sake.
- Learn about your available health care (medical and dental) options through the http://www.tricare.mil website or visit the TRICARE specialist at your nearest military medical treatment facility (MTF). Important to note: you must be enrolled in DEERS before you can use military medical or dental services.
- You're going to want to figure out where to live, too. You may be required to live on the military installation in government housing,

or not. Check with your housing office to figure out your options. You might be staying in billeting or a guesthouse until you can either find a place off the installation or until you are assigned on-installation housing. Your service member may also be eligible for a Temporary Living Expense (TLE) allowance.

Organize important papers such as birth certificates, marriage certificates, and Social Security cards. Make copies of everything. Keep the originals in a binder, and store them in a fireproof box. Keep the copies in a folder for easy access. That way, when you need them you don't have to pull the originals out of the fireproof box, and if you have to take the paperwork somewhere then you won't lose the originals.

—Debbie Milby, U.S. Army (Retired) and U.S. Army Spouse

TRANSLATING MILITARY LANGUAGE INTO ENGLISH

The military is a culture of its own. They use a lot of acronyms when they speak. You will find yourself asking your husband what they mean.

—Rebecca Roth, U.S. Air Force Spouse

When service members transition out of the military, they often find it terribly difficult to translate their skills and abilities into a language that civilian employers will fully understand. There's a flip side to that story, too.

When service members join the military, they and their families often find it terribly difficult to understand what is being said around them, at least initially. There are so many acronyms, and some of them have multiple meanings.

To further complicate matters, particularly if you happened to be stationed on a joint services installation, each branch of service has its own pot of alphabet soup. It's not just the acronyms, either. The military is full of strange, new words and unique expressions.

At first, you will feel lost, and that is a completely normal way to feel. Over time, you will come to understand what people are referring to, however. You may even catch yourself speaking in military yourself.

It will help immensely if you visit the family center on the military installation and sign up for newcomer classes. The Army, for example, has Army Family Team Building (AFTB) classes that can help you better transition into the military lifestyle. The other service branches also have similar classes through their family centers, too.

For a starter list of Military Terms and Expressions, see Appendix B.

Telling Time Military Style

Even something as simple as telling time can seem confusing. The military uses the twenty-four-hour clock, which takes a little getting used to if you haven't used it before.

For example, let's say you call the military treatment facility (MTF or military health care clinic) to schedule a doctor's appointment for yourself. The person on the other end of the phone may very well tell you you can have one of two time slots. You can come at 0730 (zero seven thirty) or you can come at 1300 (thirteen hundred hours).

Here's a military time cheat sheet to help you figure things out:

Table 1.1. Military Time

Military Time	Civilian Time
0001	12:01 am
0100	1:00 am
0200	2:00 am
0300	3:00 am
0400	4:00 am
0500	5:00 am
0600	6:00 am
0700	7:00 am
0800	8:00 am
0900	9:00 am
1000	10:00 am
1100	11:00 am
1200	12:00 Noon
1300	1:00 pm
1400	2:00 pm
1500	3:00 pm
1600	4:00 pm
1700	5:00 pm
1800	6:00 pm
1900	7:00 pm
2000	8:00 pm
2100	9:00 pm
2200	10:00 pm
2300	11:00 pm
2400	12:00 am Midnight

One notation of time you won't find on the above cheat sheet and yet you still may hear or feel the pain of at some point is o'dark thirty, which means sometime between midnight and sunrise.

Depending on your past exposure to military life, it could take you a long time to understand everything. Don't be discouraged. If you don't understand something that someone is saying, just ask that person to explain it in English to you.

You might also want to pay a visit to the installation family support center and ask them about their class for new military families. For more about military family support centers, see chapter 3, "Military Family Support."

COMMAND STRUCTURE, PAY GRADES, RANKS, AND INSIGNIAS

In the military, just as in the civilian world, everyone has a boss.

Generically speaking, in this world that boss is often referred to as someone's superior, and he works at a particular pay grade and has a specific corresponding rank. Everyone who works underneath him is often referred to as a subordinate.

You may not be fond of the hierarchical semantics here. Truthfully, who exactly is the superior or the subordinate in any given professional relationship could be a topic for heated debate, but it is safe to assume, however, that the military isn't going to change this long-standing structure any time soon.

You are not required to know about command structure, pay grades, ranks, or insignia. You're not in the military. You're not supposed to "wear" his rank as if you are, and you don't have to salute anyone. That part of this life is fairly easy for family members.

That said, it doesn't hurt to have an appreciation and a basic understanding of the world in which your loved one lives and breathes. Having such basic knowledge could save you both some professional missteps along the way.

Enlisted and Commissioned Personnel

Here are the basic enlisted and commissioned officer categories.

Junior Enlisted Personnel. Junior enlisted service members are relatively new to the military and are busy learning all kinds of new things about being in the military and about their occupational specialties. If you take a look at the Bureau of Labor Statistics, Occupational Outlook Handbook, you would see that enlisted personnel might participate in or support combat or other military operations. They also operate, maintain, and repair equipment, and they perform technical and support activities.

These have the pay grades of E-1 through E-4 in the Army and Air Force, with one exception. In the Army, both the corporal and specialist are E-4s, but the corporals are considered to be a noncommissioned officer. Specialists, on the other hand, are not. In the Marine Corps and Navy, junior enlisted personnel are service members in the pay grades of E-1 through E-3.

Non-Commission Officers (NCOs). NCOs are enlisted service members in pay grades E-5 through E-9. Army and Marine Corps corporals and Navy petty officers are E4s and are also considered noncommissioned officers.

It's a big deal when a service member becomes a noncommissioned officer. He or she has served significant time in uniform and, as an NCO, is recognized as a leader with growing responsibilities to supervise, train, and mentor others below and above them in rank. The higher the rank of an NCO, the more responsibility and authority he or she has. If they are doing their jobs correctly and opportunities permit it, junior enlisted personnel eventually evolve into senior enlisted leaders.

Warrant Officers. Warrant officers are highly specialized in their jobs. They offer subject matter and technical expertise to others. They may also serve as commanders. In the Army and Marine Corps, warrant officers are service members in the pay grades of W-1 through W-5. Naval warrant officers hold the pay grades W-2 through W-4. There aren't any warrant officers in the Air Force.

Commissioned Officers. Commissioned officers serve in the pay grades of O-1 through O-10. Many officers are generalists tasked with providing organizational leadership, administration, and management. Others may work as professionals in medicine, law, and aviation. Some commissioned officers are line officers or restricted. The former means they are capable of commanding any type of military unit, and the latter means they can only command certain types of units.

Uniforms and Insignia

Service members in uniforms are basically walking resumes. Once you know what to look for, you can tell quite a bit about that person just by looking at the type of uniform and the bling attached to it. Bling in this case means sewn patches, pinned chevrons, or medals.

You can tell whether that person is enlisted or an officer and what rank he holds. You can determine what unit or type of military unit he belongs to. You can kind of deduct how many years in service he may have based on his rank as well, but not always.

Service members also typically wear rank-specific insignia on the shoulder or collar of their uniforms.

Chevrons (*v*-shaped stripes) are worn by most enlisted personnel in every branch of service.

Bars are worn by commissioned officers. A new second lieutenant (O-1) wears a gold bar. Fun mnemonic fact: new O-1s are sometimes teased as being "butter bars."

A first lieutenant (O-2) wears a silver bar, while a captain (O-3) wears the insignia of two silver bars.

Another fun mnemonic fact: captains' insignia are often referred to as railroad tracks. Warrant officers wear striped bars. No fun facts for them.

Oak leaves are worn by commissioned officers at the Major (O-4) and Lieutenant Colonel (O-5) levels. Majors sport a gold oak leaf while Lieutenant Colonels wear the silver oak leaf.

Silver eagles are worn by commissioned officers at the Colonel (O-6) pay grade.

Stars are worn by commissioned officers at the General level. There are one-, two-, three-, and four-star generals in the military.

These emblems are worn on the military uniform, and each branch of service has multiple uniforms for different occasions, by the way. There are pretty particular rules for how insignia is worn on the uniform, and the services enforce those rules carefully.

Service, full, and dinner dress uniforms are used for more formal occasions. These are the types of uniforms that invoke the memory of a young and handsome Richard Gere in the final moments of *An Officer and a Gentleman* (circa 1982, still worth the Netflix or iTunes viewing for the eye-candy factor).

Service uniforms, on the other hand, are worn every day on the job, and working uniforms are used for nonoffice environments.

Service members address each other by their ranks. Here is a handy guide to what the ranks and insignia (what they wear on their uniforms) look like:

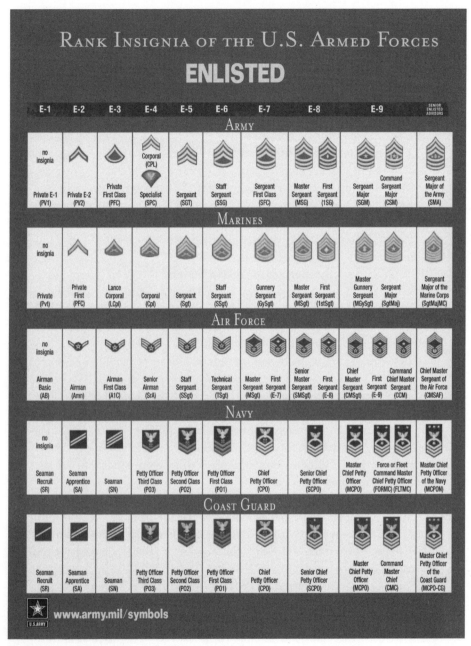

Figure 1.1. Rank Insignia of the U.S. Armed Forces
http://www.army.mil/symbols/

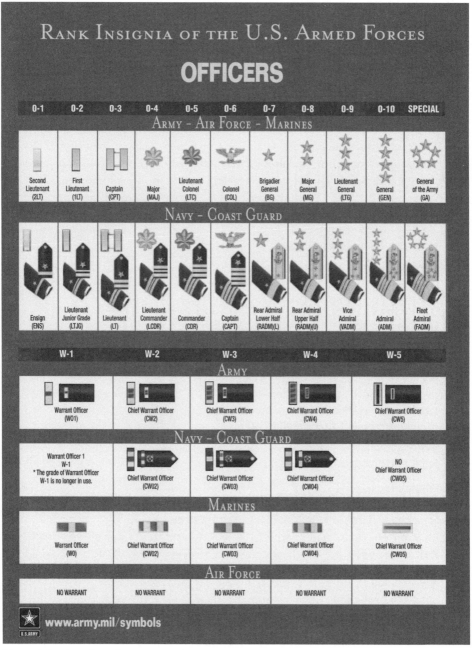

Figure 1.1. (*continued*)

COMMON MILITARY CUSTOMS AND COURTESIES

Military life is steeped in history, and each branch of service has its own traditions and customs to commemorate just about any occasion you can think of from promotions to retirements. To be sure, each branch of service has a regulation in place that can tell you all about them, and oh so much more.

Military families are often a part of those occasions. Fortunately, you don't have to look up the regulation to understand and appreciate the significance of those occasions. As a spouse or family member, you should at a minimum know how to appropriately behave at such events so that you don't appear totally clueless (read: embarrassed) at the wrong moment.

Should you be a glutton for all things protocol, however, here are the regulations:

Table 1.2.   Protocol Regulations

U.S. Army	AR 600-25	Salutes, Honors, and Visits of Courtesy
U.S. Navy	OPNAVINST 1701.7A	Social Usage and Protocol Handbook
U.S. Marines	GMK 1010	Customs and Courtesies
U.S. Air Force	AFPAM 34-1201	Guide to Protocol
U.S. Coast Guard	COMDTINST M16790.1G	Guide to Customs, Courtesies, and Protocols (chapter 12, https://www.uscg.mil/directives/cim/16000-16999/CIM_16790_1G.pdf)

White Gloves Not Required

Once upon a time, military spouses, particularly officers' wives, were expected to wear white gloves, fancy dresses, and pillbox hats. Today, thankfully, expectations are different.

You can choose to be as involved or not with your spouse's military career and all that entails. Your participation in his career is no longer a bullet point on his evaluation report, but if you want to get in a glimpse into how that used to be, watch an episode of *Astronaut Wives Club*.

That said, you are a part of the military family, and it is a proud one that honors its traditions. Etiquette and good manners never go out of style, and there will be ample occasions to apply both.

Below you'll find a short list of typical events or occasions that you might go to during your tour as a military family member.

Unit Hail and Farewells. At a unit hail and farewell, new service members and their families are welcomed by the battalion commander or other leadership while departing ones are thanked for their service and time spent with the unit. These events are wonderful opportunities for family members to meet and get to know each other. Go to them!

They are often informal gatherings, held after working hours. Food and drink may be involved. They may be held on or off the military installation at a community club, a local restaurant, someone's home, or other venue.

Those service members who are being recognized generally offer up a few words to everyone present. A unit gift, such as a plaque, is given to those service members leaving. Sometimes gag gifts are presented for fun, too. Flowers may be given to the departing spouses. Dress is typically nice causal, unless otherwise stated.

Military Balls. All branches of the military host formal military balls. Service members wear their dress blue or Class A uniforms. Female spouses and guests wear cocktail or ball-length gowns. Male spouses and guests generally wear dark suits or tuxedos.

In all things clothes related, when it comes to these events, think classy, not trashy, unless you just want to end up splashed negatively across someone's Instagram account or Facebook page.

Typically, balls are held on or around service branch birthdays in honor of the date.

Table 1.3.   Service Branch Birthdays

Service Branch	Birthday
U.S. Army	June 14
U.S. Air Force	September 18
U.S. Navy	October 13
U.S. Marine Corps	November 10

Balls generally have an agenda for the event. Cocktail hour usually happens first, often around 1700 to 1900. Some events hire a photographer to give guests the opportunity to purchase photos.

Some balls will then have a receiving line before guests are seated for dinner.

Seating may be open, or there may be assigned seating. If the latter is the case, usually a seating chart is posted at the entrance of the event, giving you the opportunity to figure out where you are supposed to sit.

Generally speaking, the head table is reserved for the command team and their spouses in attendance.

Retirement Ceremonies. When a service member retires from the military, his or her service is recognized in a formal retirement ceremony. Those who retire often do so after twenty-plus years of service, but not always. Some service members may retire earlier for other reasons.

The retirement ceremony are usually a happy occasion when the service member and his or her family are recognized and thanked officially for their service. Like nearly every other military ceremony, there is generally a set sequence of events that includes:

- opening narration
- arrival of guest of honor
- music
- posting of the colors
- invocation
- remarks
- presentation of medals
- reading of retirement orders
- presentation of retirement certificate
- presentation of flag, retired pins, and letters
- spousal appreciation (certificate and flowers given)
- guest of honor remarks (tears not uncommon!)
- closing remarks
- more music and departure of guests

Retirement ceremonies are generally followed by a party, where the guest of honor participates in a ceremonial retirement cake cutting and a toast with a refreshing beverage of choice.

Coffees and Teas. Coffees and teas are short but sweet events giving military spouses of a particular unit the opportunity to get together with one another. Coffee and/or tea is provided, along with light snacks.

Dress is usually smart casual for such a gathering. Hostess gifts are optional. Sometimes they are held on a monthly basis. Responsibility for hosting and/or cohosting the event may be rotated among spouses, or it may be routinely held at the unit senior spouse's quarters.

Spouse coffees and teas are great places to learn more about what is going on behind the scenes in your uniformed spouse's military life.

Promotion Parties. When someone in the military is promoted, it's cause for a party, a promotion party as it were. It is typically held at a local bar or someone's house, and the guest of honor is charged with supplying the food and drink. After all, he or she just got a raise.

Dining In and Dining Out. A dining in is a formal dinner function for members of a military unit. It's designed to be an event that celebrates the cohesion of a unit.

A dining out is also a formal dinner function for members of a military unit, but spouses and other guests outside the unit are also invited.

The evening's festivities are managed by the "President" (the commander or deputy commander) and "Mr./Ms./Madame Vice" (the organizer and master of ceremony) of the event. There are Rules of the Mess, a Punch Bowl Ceremony, and someone will certainly get ordered to do pushups in formal wear before the night is over.

Change of Command. When the leadership of a military unit changes, there is a change of command ceremony where the outgoing commander "passes the colors" or officially transfers the authority of the unit to the incoming commander.

It is a traditional and dignified ceremony. You don't have to be invited to attend the actual ceremony. Don't crash the after party, however, unless you have an invitation.

POW/MIA Table

At any formal dining military event you attend, you'll most likely notice a POW/MIA Table. This special table of honor is also known as the Fallen Comrade Table or the Missing Man Table. It is a small, symbolic table set for one.

There are a number of items on the table, and each one of those items has a special meaning. At some point during the course of the dinner, the host will mention it, and respect will be paid to our prisoners of war and those missing in action as they are remembered and never forgotten.

It seems as if this would go without mentioning, but just in case: *Don't sit at this table or use it as resting spot for a purse, cell phone, or programs.* It would be very inappropriate to do so.

Common Courtesies and Guidelines to Remember

- If you receive an invitation to an event that requires you to RSVP in advance of it, respond promptly and certainly by the RSVP date. If you initially decline to attend, don't change your mind later. If you accept, be sure you go barring any unavoidable and genuine emergencies.

- During formal ceremonies, don't stress out if you aren't sure when to stand or sit. Just take your cue from those around you who look like they know what they're doing.
- Dress appropriately for the occasion. Written invitations generally tell you the dress code in advance. If you aren't sure of the dress code and you know for certain it's not a formal event, dress business casual or in your Sunday best.
- Don't overindulge in alcoholic beverages. If you and/or your spouse do plan to drink, have a designated driver or call a taxi. Nothing ruins a celebration like a DWI and a loss of a budding military career or worse.
- If you are invited to an event, greet the host or hostess upon your arrival without monopolizing his or her time. Be sure you circle back to that person before you leave to offer your sincere thanks for the invitation.
- Show up on time. On time means *on time* in the military world. If you show up early to a social event, you'll most likely be in the way as final preparations are underway.
- During any ceremony, stand when colors (the flags) are posted and when the National Anthem is played.
- Stand as a courtesy when foreign nation anthems are played, too.
- If there is a receiving line at an event, keep the line moving. Smile, grin, greet, shake hands, and then move on. This isn't the time to have lengthy conversations, and don't make the mistake of carrying a drink with you through the line, either.
- Children are a big part of the military family, but their presence isn't always appropriate at certain events, depending, of course, on their ages and the event in question. If you want to bring your children with you on some occasion, don't assume your kids are welcome to attend. Ask first, and have a good list of potential babysitters ready just in case.

2

MILITARY MONEY AND BENEFITS

Money may not make the world go around, but it certainly helps to pay the rent and put food on the table.

As a new military family member, you should understand that the concept of *financial readiness* is a pretty big deal in this world, and it's easy to understand why, too.

When military families are able to pay their bills on time, save and invest for the future, and enjoy a satisfying quality of life, then service members can better focus on the job of safeguarding the free world.

This is also known as *mission readiness*. As you might imagine, it is of the utmost importance to the DoD, which has placed much effort and funding into teaching those in uniform and their families the value of financial literacy.

It doesn't hurt to state the obvious here. Personal financial mismanagement, the polar opposite of financial management, can be disastrous to your family's quality of life and to the service member's military career.

According to the 2015 Military Compensation and Retirement Modernization Commission Final Report, "a bad credit report or debt-collection action, or other financial problem can be devastating for a Service member's career and can affect the mission readiness of a unit, which often cannot use a service member who has lost a security clearance due to financial problems."[1]

Interesting to note, the report also mentions financial issues were the fourth highest-ranking reason for the loss of security clearances.

Security clearances, if you're not already aware, are often necessary for many service members in the military to do their jobs. They are also costly and extremely time consuming to obtain. They also make great bullet points to add to a service member's resume for postuniform job-hunting purposes.

NEWBIES' GUIDE TO MILITARY
PAY AND ALLOWANCES

In order to effectively manage your finances, however, you need to have a good understanding of them in the first place.

Newbie, be warned. There's a lot to learn here. Your pay and allowances could vary as you go through different experiences in military life. You have to stay on top of it because one small mistake on someone's part could result in a nasty little surprise for you when you can least afford it. No one likes nasty little surprises. They tend to snowball into nasty big ones.

The key to preventing that from happening, on your part anyway, is to learn as much as you can about due pay and benefits.

You can find out everything you ever wanted to know by visiting the Defense Finance and Accounting System (DFAS) website at http://www .dfas.mil, click on Military Members, and then Pay and Allowances. The DoD's Military Compensation site, http://militarypay.defense.gov, is also very helpful.

For the purpose of basic training, however, let's go over the essential need-to-know information now.

DFAS is the organization that processes the pay that your service member works hard for day in and day out. Anyone who serves in uniform or who works for the DoD should have an online myPay account where they can keep track of what goes in and what goes out. Service members usually create a myPay account early in their uniformed careers.

Should you ever work for the federal government yourself, you will get to create and use your own myPay account, too.

Service members generally get paid twice a month, once on the first and again on the fifteenth. Pay is usually direct deposited into a designated bank account of your service member's choice.

Leave and Earnings Statements (LES) detail the payment transaction and can either be mailed to the service member routinely or accessed online through the myPay account. It's important to know how to read an LES and to truly understand all the information it is telling you. See Understanding the Leave and Earnings Statement, which appears later in this chapter.

Military pay consists of a base pay plus other allowances and special pays, depending on what the service member is doing in his or her career at the time.

Base pay is considered to be the centerpiece of the total compensation package. It is based upon rank and time in service. See figure 2.1 (basic pay charts) for more information.

Suffice it to say, rank has its privileges. An enlisted E1, E2, or E3 in any branch of service makes less than a commissioned officer who is an O1, O2, or O3.

Every year, the DoD unveils a new pay chart for all. You can access pay charts from 1949 to the present day on the DFAS website. The exact link is: http://www.dfas.mil/militarymembers/payentitlements/military -pay-charts.html.

Pay raises typically happen annually. In recent years, however, they have not been significant.

According to the DoD, annual military pay raises are linked to the increase in private sector wages. In 2016, service members received a 1.3 percent pay raise and in 2015, they received a 1 percent raise.

Where those linked numbers are coming from isn't always clear. For example, employees in the United States are predicted to see a 3 percent salary increase in 2016, a far cry from a 1.3 percent for the military.[2] To be fair, however, there are many valuable benefits that could compensate for the lack of dollar-for-dollar matching. Stay tuned.

The bottom line here is simple. Make a diligent effort to keep up with news about changing military pay and benefits because change is definitely here to stay on those fronts.

You should also understand that some of the money your service member earns is taxed and some is not. Base pay, for instance, is taxable at both the federal and state levels, with some state exceptions.

For example, military members claiming residency in Arkansas, Kentucky, Minnesota, New Mexico, and Oklahoma may have all or part of their qualifying military pay exempt from state income taxes. Contact the state's Tax Commission or Department of Revenue for more information.[3]

More than just base pay is earned here, however, and those additional earnings may or may not be taxable at the federal and/or state level depending on what they are specifically.

Before we go further into detail here, it would be wise to remind you that big-picture changes to the existing military pay system are on the horizon that may very well affect your family in some way.

The current Secretary of Defense Ashton Carter and the Pentagon's top officials have been busy designing the "Force of the Future," which will reportedly fundamentally change how the military recruits, pays, promotes, and manages its 1.3 million troops.[4]

As a result, there may ultimately be new basic tables for high-demand career fields. For example, those who work in cybersecurity and other high-tech fields may see more money in their paychecks. Additionally,

Gr.	2 or less	Over 2	Over 3	Over 4	Over 6	Over 8	Over 10	Over 12	Over 14	Over 16	Over 18
O-10											
O-9											
O-8	9,946.20	10,272.00	10,488.30	10,548.60	10,818.60	11,269.20	11,373.90	11,802.00	11,924.70	12,293.40	12,827.10
O-7	8,264.40	8,648.40	8,826.00	8,967.30	9,222.90	9,475.80	9,767.70	10,059.00	10,351.20	11,269.20	12,043.80
O-6	6,267.00	6,885.30	7,337.10	7,337.10	7,365.00	7,680.90	7,722.30	7,722.30	8,161.20	8,937.00	9,392.70
O-5	5,224.50	5,885.70	6,292.80	6,369.60	6,624.00	6,776.10	7,110.30	7,356.00	7,673.10	8,158.50	8,388.90
O-4	4,507.80	5,218.20	5,566.50	5,643.90	5,967.00	6,313.80	6,745.80	7,081.50	7,314.90	7,449.30	7,526.70
O-3	3,963.60	4,492.80	4,849.20	5,287.20	5,540.70	5,818.80	5,998.20	6,293.70	6,448.20	6,448.20	6,448.20
O-2	3,424.50	3,900.30	4,491.90	4,643.70	4,739.40	4,739.40	4,739.40	4,739.40	4,739.40	4,739.40	4,739.40
O-1	2,972.40	3,093.90	3,740.10	3,740.10	3,740.10	3,740.10	3,740.10	3,740.10	3,740.10	3,740.10	3,740.10
O-3E				5,287.20	5,540.70	5,818.80	5,998.20	6,293.70	6,543.30	6,686.70	6,881.40
O-2E				4,643.70	4,739.40	4,890.30	5,145.00	5,341.80	5,488.50	5,488.50	5,488.50
O-1E				3,740.10	3,993.60	4,141.50	4,292.40	4,440.60	4,643.70	4,643.70	4,643.70
W-5											
W-4	4,095.90	4,406.10	4,532.40	4,656.90	4,871.10	5,083.20	5,298.00	5,620.80	5,904.00	6,173.40	6,393.90
W-3	3,740.40	3,896.40	4,056.30	4,108.80	4,276.20	4,605.90	4,949.10	5,110.80	5,297.70	5,490.30	5,836.50
W-2	3,309.90	3,622.80	3,719.40	3,785.40	4,000.20	4,333.80	4,499.10	4,661.70	4,860.90	5,016.30	5,157.30
W-1	2,905.50	3,218.10	3,302.10	3,479.70	3,690.00	3,999.60	4,144.20	4,346.10	4,545.00	4,701.60	4,845.30
E-9							4,948.80	5,060.70	5,202.30	5,368.20	5,536.20
E-8						4,050.90	4,230.00	4,341.00	4,473.90	4,618.20	4,878.00
E-7	2,816.10	3,073.50	3,191.40	3,347.10	3,468.90	3,678.00	3,795.60	4,004.70	4,178.70	4,297.50	4,423.80
E-6	2,435.70	2,680.20	2,798.40	2,913.60	3,033.60	3,303.30	3,408.60	3,612.30	3,674.40	3,719.70	3,772.50
E-5	2,231.40	2,381.40	2,496.60	2,614.20	2,797.80	2,989.80	3,147.60	3,166.20	3,166.20	3,166.20	3,166.20
E-4	2,046.00	2,150.40	2,267.10	2,382.00	2,483.40	2,483.40	2,483.40	2,483.40	2,483.40	2,483.40	2,483.40
E-3	1,847.10	1,963.20	2,082.00	2,082.00	2,082.00	2,082.00	2,082.00	2,082.00	2,082.00	2,082.00	2,082.00
E-2	1,756.50	1,756.50	1,756.50	1,756.50	1,756.50	1,756.50	1,756.50	1,756.50	1,756.50	1,756.50	1,756.50
E-1	1566.90										

Notes:
1. Basic pay for an O-7 to O-10 is limited by Level II of the Executive Schedule which is $15,125.10. Basic pay for O-6 and below is limited by Level V of the Executive Schedule in effect during 2016, which is $12,516.60.
2. While serving as Chairman, Joint Chief of Staff/Vice Chairman, Joint Chief of Staff, Chief of Navy Operations, Commandant of the Marine Corps, Army/Air Force Chief of Staff, Chief of the National Guard Bureau Commander of a unified or specified combatant command, basic pay is $21,147.30. (See note 1 above).
3. Applicable to O-1 to O-3 with at least 4 years and 1 day of active duty or more than 1460 points as a warrant and/or enlisted member. See Department of Defense Financial Management Regulations for more detailed explanation on who is eligible for this special basic pay rate.
4. For the Master Chief Petty Officer of the Navy, Chief Master Sergeant of the AF, Sergeant Major of the Army or Marine Corps or Senior Enlisted Advisor of the JCS, basic pay is $7,997.10. Combat Zone Tax Exclusion for O-1 and above is based on this basic pay rate plus Hostile Fire Pay/Imminent Danger Pay which is $225.00.
5. Applicable to E-1 with 4 months or more of active duty. Basic pay for an E-1 with less than 4 months of active duty is $1,040.70.
6. Basic pay rate for Academy Cadets/Midshipmen and ROTC members/applicants is $1,040.70.

Figure 2.1. Basic Pay Charts
http://www.dfas.mil/militarymembers/payentitlements/military-pay-charts.html

BASIC PAY—EFFECTIVE JANUARY 1, 2016

Pay Grade	Over 20	Over 22	Over 24	Over 26	Over 28	Over 30	Over 32	Over 34	Over 36	Over 38	Over 40
O-10[1]	16,072.20	16,150.50	16,486.80	17,071.50	17,071.50	17,925.30	17,925.30	18,821.10	18,821.10	19,762.50	19,762.50
O-9[1]	14,056.80	14,259.90	14,552.10	15,062.40	15,062.40	15,816.00	15,816.00	16,606.80	16,606.80	17,436.90	17,436.90
O-8[1]	13,319.10	13,647.30	13,647.30	13,647.30	13,647.30	13,989.00	13,989.00	14,338.50	14,338.50	14,338.50	14,338.50
O-7[1]	12,043.80	12,043.80	12,043.80	12,105.60	12,105.60	12,347.70	12,347.70	12,347.70	12,347.70	12,347.70	12,347.70
O-6[2]	9,847.80	10,106.70	10,369.20	10,877.70	10,877.70	11,094.90	11,094.90	11,094.90	11,094.90	11,094.90	11,094.90
O-5	8,617.20	8,876.40	8,876.40	8,876.40	8,876.40	8,876.40	8,876.40	8,876.40	8,876.40	8,876.40	8,876.40
O-4	7,526.70	7,526.70	7,526.70	7,526.70	7,526.70	7,526.70	7,526.70	7,526.70	7,526.70	7,526.70	7,526.70
O-3	6,448.20	6,448.20	6,448.20	6,448.20	6,448.20	6,448.20	6,448.20	6,448.20	6,448.20	6,448.20	6,448.20
O-2	4,739.40	4,739.40	4,739.40	4,739.40	4,739.40	4,739.40	4,739.40	4,739.40	4,739.40	4,739.40	4,739.40
O-1	3,740.10	3,740.10	3,740.10	3,740.10	3,740.10	3,740.10	3,740.10	3,740.10	3,740.10	3,740.10	3,740.10
O-3[3]	6,881.40	6,881.40	6,881.40	6,881.40	6,881.40	6,881.40	6,881.40	6,881.40	6,881.40	6,881.40	6,881.40
O-2[3]	5,488.50	5,488.50	5,488.50	5,488.50	5,488.50	5,488.50	5,488.50	5,488.50	5,488.50	5,488.50	5,488.50
O-1[3]	4,643.70	4,643.70	4,643.70	4,643.70	4,643.70	4,643.70	4,643.70	4,643.70	4,643.70	4,643.70	4,643.70
W-5	7,283.10	7,652.40	7,927.50	8,232.30	8,232.30	8,644.50	8,644.50	9,076.20	9,076.20	9,530.70	9,530.70
W-4	6,608.70	6,924.60	7,184.10	7,480.20	7,480.20	7,629.60	7,629.60	7,629.60	7,629.60	7,629.60	7,629.60
W-3	6,070.50	6,210.30	6,359.10	6,561.60	6,561.60	6,561.60	6,561.60	6,561.60	6,561.60	6,561.60	6,561.60
W-2	5,325.90	5,436.60	5,524.50	5,524.50	5,524.50	5,524.50	5,524.50	5,524.50	5,524.50	5,524.50	5,524.50
W-1	5,020.50	5,020.50	5,020.50	5,020.50	5,020.50	5,020.50	5,020.50	5,020.50	5,020.50	5,020.50	5,020.50
E-9[4]	5,804.70	6,032.10	6,270.90	6,636.90	6,636.90	6,968.40	6,968.40	7,317.00	7,317.00	7,683.30	7,683.30
E-8	5,009.40	5,233.80	5,358.00	5,664.00	5,664.00	5,777.70	5,777.70	5,777.70	5,777.70	5,777.70	5,777.70
E-7	4,472.70	4,637.10	4,725.30	5,061.30	5,061.30	5,061.30	5,061.30	5,061.30	5,061.30	5,061.30	5,061.30
E-6	3,772.50	3,772.50	3,772.50	3,772.50	3,772.50	3,772.50	3,772.50	3,772.50	3,772.50	3,772.50	3,772.50
E-5	3,166.20	3,166.20	3,166.20	3,166.20	3,166.20	3,166.20	3,166.20	3,166.20	3,166.20	3,166.20	3,166.20
E-4	2,483.40	2,483.40	2,483.40	2,483.40	2,483.40	2,483.40	2,483.40	2,483.40	2,483.40	2,483.40	2,483.40
E-3	2,082.00	2,082.00	2,082.00	2,082.00	2,082.00	2,082.00	2,082.00	2,082.00	2,082.00	2,082.00	2,082.00
E-2	1,756.50	1,756.50	1,756.50	1,756.50	1,756.50	1,756.50	1,756.50	1,756.50	1,756.50	1,756.50	1,756.50

Notes:

1. Basic pay for an O-7 to O-10 is limited by Level II of the Executive Schedule which is $15,125.10. Basic pay for O-6 and below is limited by Level V of the Executive Schedule in effect during 2016, which is $12,516.60.
2. While serving as Chairman, Joint Chief of Staff/Vice Chairman, Joint Chief of Staff, Chief of Navy Operations, Commandant of the Marine Corps, Army/Air Force Chief of Staff, Chief of the National Guard Bureau, or Commander of a unified or specified combatant command, basic pay is $21,147.30. *(See note 1 above).*
3. Applicable to O-1 to O-3 with at least 4 years and 1 day of active duty or more than 1460 points as a warrant and/or enlisted member. See Department of Defense Financial Management Regulations for more detailed explanation on who is eligible for this special pay rate.
4. For the Master Chief Petty Officer of the Navy, Chief Master Sergeant of the AF, Sergeant Major of the Army or Marine Corps, Senior Enlisted Advisor to the Chief of the National Guard Bureau, or Senior Enlisted Advisor of the JCS, basic pay is $7,997.10. Combat Zone Tax Exclusion for O-1 and above is based on this basic pay rate plus Hostile Fire Pay/Imminent Danger Pay which is $225.00.
5. Applicable to E-1 with 4 months or more of active duty. Basic pay for an E-1 with less than 4 months of active duty is $1,449.00.
6. Basic pay rate for Academy Cadets/Midshipmen and ROTC members/applicants is $1,040.70.

ALLOWANCES

Basic Allowance for Housing RC/Transient (January 1, 2016)

Pay Grade	Partial	Without Dependent	With Dependent	Differential
0-10	$50.70	$1,616.70	$1,988.70	$333.60
0-9	$50.70	$1,616.70	$1,988.70	$333.60
0-8	$50.70	$1,616.70	$1,988.70	$333.60
0-7	$50.70	$1,616.70	$1,988.70	$333.60
0-6	$39.60	$1,482.30	$1,790.10	$283.50
0-5	$33.00	$1,427.40	$1,725.90	$274.20
0-4	$26.70	$1,322.40	$1,521.00	$182.40
0-3	$22.20	$1,060.50	$1,258.50	$182.10
0-2	$17.70	$840.30	$1,074.00	$214.80
0-1	$13.20	$721.20	$961.20	$232.20
03E	$22.20	$1,144.50	$1,353.00	$190.80
02E	$17.70	$973.50	$1,220.70	$228.30
01E	$13.20	$846.60	$1,128.30	$267.60
W-5	$25.20	$1,344.00	$1,469.10	$114.00
W-4	$25.20	$1,193.10	$1,346.70	$140.40
W-3	$20.70	$1,003.50	$1,234.50	$211.80
W-2	$15.90	$890.40	$1,134.00	$223.80
W-1	$13.80	$746.70	$981.90	$216.60
E-9	$18.60	$979.80	$1,292.10	$285.90
E-8	$15.30	$900.30	$1,191.90	$267.90
E-7	$12.00	$829.80	$1,106.10	$310.20
E-6	$9.90	$766.80	$1,021.80	$300.00
E-5	$8.70	$689.70	$919.50	$255.30
E-4	$8.10	$600.00	$799.20	$220.50
E-3	$7.80	$557.70	$743.10	$180.90
E-2	$7.20	$531.60	$708.30	$241.50
E-1	$6.90	$531.60	$708.30	$285.90

Family Separation Allowance

All Pay Grades: $250

Basic Allowance for Subsistence (Effective January 1, 2016)	Family Subsistence Supplemental Allowance (Effective October 1, 2010)
Officers: $253.63	All Pay Grades
Enlisted: $368.29	Not to Exceed $1100.00

Clothing Allowances (Effective October 1, 2015)

Standard Initial Clothing Allowance (Enlisted Members Only)

	Army		Navy		Air Force		Marine Corps	
	Male	Female	Male	Female	Male	Female	Male	Female
	1,643.45	1,888.07	1,797.42	1,982.74	1,389.18	1,597.93	2,007.82	1,945.65

Cash Clothing Replacement Allowance (Enlisted Members Only)

	Army		Navy		Air Force		Marine Corps	
	Male	Female	Male	Female	Male	Female	Male	Female
Basic	327.60	349.20	320.40	327.60	248.40	252.00	403.20	392.40
Standard	468.00	496.80	457.20	468.00	352.80	360.00	601.20	576.00
Special	0	0	648.00	669.60	0	0	0	0

Civilian Clothing Allowance

Type of Duty	Initial	Replacement	15 days in 30 days period	30 days in 36 month period
Permanent	1,022.40	340.80	0	0
Temporary	0	0	340.80	681.60

Personal Money Allowance (Monthly Amount)

1. While serving as Chairman or Vice Chairman of the JCS, or Army or Air Force CS, CNO, or CMC	$333.33
2. Senior Member of the Military Staff Committee of the U.N.	$225.00
3. General or Admiral	$183.33
4. Lieutenant General Vice Admiral	$41.67
5. Senior Enlisted Member of a Military Service	$166.67

For other pays or specific requirements for the pay cited in this table, go to the web at:
http://www.dtic.mil/comptroller/fmr/07a/index.html

INCENTIVE AND SPECIAL PAYS

Aviation Career Incentive Pay

Years of Aviation Service

2 or less	Over 2	Over 3	Over 4	Over 6	Over 14	Over 22	Over 23	Over 24	Over 25
125.00	156.00	188.00	206.00	650.00	840.00	585.00	495.00	385.00	250.00

Career Enlisted Flyer Incentive Pay

Years of Aviation Service

4 or less	Over 4	Over 8	Over 14
150.00	225.00	350.00	400.00

Hazardous Duty Incentive Pay (Crew Member- Non-AWAC)

Pay Grade	Amount	Pay Grade	Amount	Pay Grade	Amount	Pay Grade	Amount
O-10	150.00	W-5	250.00	E-9	240.00	E-4	165.00
O-9	150.00	W-4	225.00	E-8	240.00	E-3	150.00
O-8	150.00	W-3	175.00	E-7	240.00	E-2	150.00
O-7	150.00	W-2	150.00	E-6	215.00	E-1	150.00
O-6	250.00	W-1	150.00	E-5	190.00		

Hazardous Duty Incentive Pay (Non-Crew Member)

ALL GRADES – 150.00

Diving Pay

ALL GRADES – 150.00

Officers – 240.00 (Max)   Enlisted – 340.00 (Max)

Imminent Danger Pay/Hostile Fire Pay

ALL GRADES – 225.00

HDIP (Parachute, Flight Deck, Demolition, & Others)

All Grades – 150.00
(Member qualified for **HALO Pay** – 225.00).

COMBAT ZONE TAX EXCLUSION

Basic pay for the MCPO of the Navy, CMSgt of the AF, Sergeant Major of the Army or Marine Corps, basic pay is $7,816.20. Combat Zone Tax Exclusion for O-1 and above is based on this basic pay rate plus HFP/IDP ($225).

For other pays or specific requirements for the pays cited in this table, go to the web at:
http://www.dtic.mil/comptroller/fmr/07a/index.html

Submarine Duty Incentive Pay (Effective October 1, 2011)

Cumulative Years of Service

Pay Grade	2 or less	Over 2	Over 3	Over 4	Over 6	Over 8	Over 10	Over 14	Over 16	Over 18
O-6	595.00									835.00
O-5	595.00								835.00	
O-4	365.00			525.00	595.00	705.00		790.00		
O-3	355.00			510.00	595.00	705.00		790.00		
O-2	305.00						425.00			
O-1	230.00						425.00			
W-5	285.00	375.00		425.00						
W-4	285.00	375.00		425.00						
W-3	285.00	375.00		425.00				425.00		
W-2	285.00	375.00		425.00				425.00		
W-1	285.00	375.00		425.00						
E-9	425.00									600.00
E-8	415.00									550.00
E-7	405.00									
E-6	155.00	170.00	175.00	300.00	325.00	375.00				
E-5	140.00	155.00		250.00	275.00					
E-4	80.00	95.00	100.00	245.00						
E-3	80.00	90.00	95.00		90.00					
E-2	75.00	90.00								
E-1	75.00									

Submarine Duty Incentive Pay for O-7 through O-10 is $355.00

MONTHLY CAREER SEA PAY—(NAVY AND MARINE CORPS)—EFFECTIVE MAY 1, 2014

Cumulative Years of Sea Duty

Pay Grade	1 or less	Over 1	Over 2	Over 3	Over 4	Over 5	Over 6	Over 7	Over 8	Over 9	Over 10	Over 11	Over 12	Over 13	Over 14	Over 16	Over 18	Over 20
O-6	100	100	100	394	400	400	419	450	463	494	506	525	544	544	569	594	625	669
O-5	100	100	100	394	394	394	394	400	431	438	456	463	463	463	500	525	550	594
O-4	100	100	100	325	331	350	356	375	388	388	394	394	419	419	475	494	506	525
O-3	100	100	100	263	281	325	331	344	356	375	394	394	419	419	456	475	494	506
O-2	100	100	100	263	281	325	331	344	356	375	394	394	419	419	438	456	475	494
O-1	100	100	100	263	281	325	331	344	356	375	394	394	419	419	438	456	475	494
W-5	210	210	210	263	300	506	544	544	544	544	613	656	700	700	750	750	750	750
W-4	210	210	210	263	300	506	544	544	544	544	613	656	700	700	750	750	750	750
W-3	210	210	210	263	300	475	494	500	506	544	613	656	700	700	744	744	750	750
W-2	210	210	210	263	300	456	463	463	475	544	594	594	656	656	700	700	700	700
W-1	180	190	195	263	300	306	350	438	475	525	569	569	594	594	631	656	656	656
E-9	135	135	160	381	400	438	438	469	688	700	700	713	725	750	750	750	750	750
E-8	135	135	160	381	400	438	438	469	688	700	700	713	725	750	750	750	750	750
E-7	135	135	160	381	400	438	438	469	688	700	700	713	725	750	750	750	750	750
E-6	135	135	160	350	375	394	406	438	638	656	656	656	675	694	713	731	638	638
E-5	70	80	160	350	375	394	406	438	638	638	638	638	638	638	638	638	638	638
E-4	70	80	160	350	363	363	363	363	488	488	488	488	488	488	488	488	488	488
E-3	50	60	100	125	125	125	125	125	125	125	125	125	125	125	125	125	125	125
E-2	50	60	75	94	94	94	94	94	94	94	94	94	94	94	94	94	94	94
E-1	50	50	50	63	63	63	63	63	63	63	63	63	63	63	63	63	63	63

Career Sea Pay-Premium is $200 per month. Career Sea Pay-Premium is not paid to grades E5 through E9 over 8 years of cumulative sea duty. Career Sea Pay-Premium is included in their Career Sea Pay.

MONTHLY CAREER SEA PAY—EFFECTIVE MAY 1, 1988 (AIR FORCE MEMBERS)

Cumulative Years of Sea Duty

Pay Grade	1 or less	Over 1	Over 2	Over 3	Over 4	Over 5	Over 6	Over 7	Over 8	Over 9	Over 10	Over 11	Over 12	Over 13	Over 14	Over 16	Over 18	Over 20
O-6				225	230		240	255	265	280	290	300	310		325	340	355	380
O-5				225				230	245	250	260	265			285	300	315	340
O-4				185	190	200	205	215	220		225		240		270	280	290	300
O-3				150	160	185	190	195	205	215	225		240		260	270	290	290
O-2				150	160	185	190	195	205	215	225		240		250	260	270	280
O-1				150	160	185	190	195	205	215	225		240		250	260	270	280
E-9	100		120	175	190	350		375	390	400		410	420	450	475	520		
E-8	100		120	175	190	350		375	390	400		410	420	450	475	500	520	
E-7	100		120	175	190	350		375	390	400		410	420	450	475	500		
E-6	100		120	150	170	315	325	350		365			380	395	410	425	450	
E-5	50	60	120	150	170	315	325	350										
E-4	50	60	120	150	160													

MONTHLY CAREER SEA PAY—EFFECTIVE OCTOBER 1, 2002 (ARMY MEMBERS)

Cumulative Years of Sea Duty

Pay Grade	1 or less	Over 1	Over 2	Over 3	Over 4	Over 5	Over 6	Over 7	Over 8	Over 9	Over 10	Over 11	Over 12	Over 13	Over 14	Over 16	Over 18	Over 20
O-6				225	230		240	255	265	280	290	300	310		325	340	355	380
O-5				225				230	245	250	260	265			285	300	315	340
O-4				185	190	200	205	215	220		225		240		270	280	290	300
O-3				150	160	185	190	195	205	215	225		240		260	270	280	290
O-2				150	160	185	190	195	205	215	225		240		250	260	270	280
O-1				150	160	185	190	195	205	215	225		240		250	260	270	280
W-5	210			310	338	506	534				590	625	660		730			
W-4	210			310	338	506	534				590	625	660		730			
W-3	210			310	338	478	492	499	506	534	590	625	660		695			
W-2	210			310	338	464	471	478	478	534	576		625					
W-1	182	189	196	310	338	345	380	450	478	520	555							
E-9	130		156	328	347	425		458	477	490		503	516	555	588	620	646	
E-8	130		156	328	347	425		458	477	490		503	516	555	588	620	646	
E-7	130		156	328	347	425		458	477	490		503	516	555	588	620		
E-6	130		156	295	321	380	393			445			464	484	503	523	555	
E-5	65	78	156	295	321	380	393	425										
E-4	65	78	156	295	308		190											
E-3	50	60	120	150	160	170												
E-2	50	60	120	150	160	170												
E-1	50	60	120	150	160													

SPECIAL PAYS FOR HEALTH PROFESSIONAL OFFICERS

Variable Special Pay (Medical Officers)

Pay Grade	Under 3	3 But Less Than 6	6 But Less Than 8	8 But Less Than 10	10 But Less Than 12	12 But Less Than 14	14 But Less Than 18	18 But Less Than 22	22 and Over
Intern	100.00								
Thru O-6		416.66	1,000.00	958.33	916.66	833.33	750.00	666.66	583.33
Above O-6	583.33								

For specific requirements for the pay cited in this table, go to the web at: http://www.dtic.mil/comptroller/fmr/07a/index.html

Variable Special Pay (VSP) (Dental Officers)

Pay Grade	Under 3	3 But Less Than 6	6 But Less Than 8	8 But Less Than 12	12 But Less Than 14	14 But Less Than 18	18 & Over
Intern	250.00						
Thru O-6		583.33	583.33	1,000.00	833.33	750.00	666.67
Above O-6	583.33						

Board Certified Pay Special Pay (Medical and Dental Officers)

Pay Grade	Under 10	10 But Less Than 12	12 But Less Than 14	14 But Less Than 18	18 & Over
All Grades	208.33	291.66	333.33	416.66	500.00

Additional Special Pay (ASP) (Dental Officers) (effective April 24, 2008)

Pay Grade	Under 3	3 But Less Than 10	10 & Over
All Grades	10,000.00	12,000.00	15,000.00

Incentive Special Pay (Medical Officers)

Specialty	Annual Amt	Specialty	Annual Amt	Specialty	Annual Amt	Specialty	Annual Amt
Aerospace Med	20,000.00	General surgery	29,000.00	Otolaryngology	30,000.00	Subspecialty Category I	36,000.00
Anesthesiology	36,000.00	Internal medicine	20,000.00	Pathology	20,000.00	Subspecialty Category II	28,000.00
Cardiology	36,000.00	Neurology	20,000.00	Pediatrics	20,000.00	Subspecialty Category III	23,000.00
Dermatology	20,000.00	Neurosurgery	36,000.00	Phys and Prev/Occ Med	20,000.00	Subspecialty Category IV	20,000.00
Emergency Med	26,000.00	OB/GYN	31,000.00	Psychiatry	20,000.00	Subspecialty Category V	36,000.00
Family practice	20,000.00	Ophthalmology	28,000.00	Pulmonary/IM-Critical Care	23,000.00	Urology	28,000.00
Gastroenterology	26,000.00	Orthopedics	36,000.00	Radiology	36,000.00		

Multiyear Retention Bonus (Dental Officers)				
	Level 1	Level 2	Level 3	Level 4
4 Year Agreement	50,000.00	40,000.00	35,000.00	25,000.00
3 Year Agreement	38,000.00	30,000.00	27,000.00	19,000.00
2 Year Agreement	25,000.00	20,000.00	18,000.00	13,000.00

DRILL PAY—EFFECTIVE JANUARY 1, 2016

Cumulative Years of Service

Pay Grade	2 or less	Over 2	Over 3	Over 4	Over 6	Over 8	Over 10	Over 12	Over 14	Over 16	Over 18	Over 20
O-7	8,264.40	8,648.40	8,826.00	8,967.30	9,222.90	9,475.80	9,767.70	10,059.00	10,351.20	11,269.20	12,043.80	12,043.80
1 Drill	275.48	288.28	294.2	298.91	307.43	315.86	325.59	335.3	345.04	375.64	401.46	401.46
4 Drills	1101.92	1153.12	1176.8	1195.64	1229.72	1263.44	1302.36	1341.2	1380.16	1502.56	1605.84	1605.84
O-6	6,267.00	6,885.30	7,337.10	7,337.10	7,365.00	7,680.90	7,722.30	7,722.30	8,161.20	8,937.00	9,392.70	9,847.80
1 Drill	208.90	229.51	244.57	244.57	245.50	256.03	257.41	257.41	272.04	297.90	313.09	328.26
4 Drills	835.60	918.04	978.28	978.28	982.00	1,024.12	1,029.64	1,029.64	1,088.16	1,191.60	1,252.36	1,313.04
O-5	5,224.50	5,885.70	6,292.80	6,369.60	6,624.00	6,776.10	7,110.30	7,356.00	7,673.10	8,158.50	8,388.90	8,617.20
1 Drill	174.15	196.19	209.76	212.32	220.80	225.87	237.01	245.20	255.77	271.95	279.63	287.24
4 Drills	696.60	784.76	839.04	849.28	883.20	903.48	948.04	980.80	1,023.08	1,087.80	1,118.52	1,148.96
O-4	4,507.80	5,218.20	5,566.50	5,643.90	5,967.00	6,313.80	6,745.80	7,081.50	7,314.90	7,449.30	7,526.70	7,526.70
1 Drill	150.26	173.94	185.55	188.13	198.90	210.46	224.86	236.05	243.83	248.31	250.89	250.89
4 Drills	601.04	695.76	742.20	752.52	795.60	841.84	899.44	944.20	975.32	993.24	1,003.56	1,003.56
O-3	3,963.60	4,492.80	4,849.20	5,287.20	5,540.70	5,818.80	5,998.20	6,293.70	6,448.20	6,448.20	6,448.20	6,448.20
1 Drill	132.12	149.76	161.64	176.24	184.69	193.96	199.94	209.79	214.94	214.94	214.94	214.94
4 Drills	528.48	599.04	646.56	704.96	738.76	775.84	799.76	839.16	859.76	859.76	859.76	859.76
O-2	3,424.50	3,900.30	4,491.90	4,643.70	4,739.40	4,739.40	4,739.40	4,739.40	4,739.40	4,739.40	4,739.40	4,739.40
1 Drill	114.15	130.01	149.73	154.79	157.98	157.98	157.98	157.98	157.98	157.98	157.98	157.98
4 Drills	456.60	520.04	598.92	619.16	631.92	631.92	631.92	631.92	631.92	631.92	631.92	631.92
O-1	2,972.40	3,093.90	3,740.10	3,740.10	3,740.10	3,740.10	3,740.10	3,740.10	3,740.10	3,740.10	3,740.10	3,740.10
1 Drill	99.08	103.13	124.67	124.67	124.67	124.67	124.67	124.67	124.67	124.67	124.67	124.67
4 Drills	396.32	412.52	498.68	498.68	498.68	498.68	498.68	498.68	498.68	498.68	498.68	498.68
O-3E				5,287.20	5,540.70	5,818.80	5,998.20	6,293.70	6,543.30	6,686.70	6,881.40	6,881.40
1 Drill				176.24	184.69	193.96	199.94	209.79	218.11	222.89	229.38	229.38
4 Drills				704.96	738.76	775.84	799.76	839.16	872.44	891.56	917.52	917.52
O-2E				4,643.70	4,739.40	4,890.30	5,145.00	5,341.80	5,488.50	5,488.50	5,488.50	5,488.50
1 Drill				154.79	157.98	163.01	171.50	178.06	182.95	182.95	182.95	182.95
4 Drills				619.16	631.92	652.04	686.00	712.24	731.80	731.80	731.80	731.80
O-1E				3,740.10	3,993.60	4,141.50	4,292.40	4,440.60	4,643.70	4,643.70	4,643.70	4,643.70
1 Drill				124.67	133.12	138.05	143.08	148.02	154.79	154.79	154.79	154.79
4 Drills				498.68	532.48	552.20	572.32	592.08	619.16	619.16	619.16	619.16

DRILL PAY—EFFECTIVE JANUARY 1, 2016

Cumulative Years of Service

Pay Grade	Over 22	Over 24	Over 26	Over 28	Over 30	Over 32	Over 34	Over 36	Over 38	Over 40
O-7	12,043.80	12,043.80	12,105.60	12,105.60	12,347.70	12,347.70	12,347.70	12,347.70	12,347.70	12,347.70
1 Drill	401.46	401.46	403.52	403.52	411.59	411.59	411.59	411.59	411.59	411.59
4 Drills	1605.84	1605.84	1614.08	1614.08	1646.36	1646.36	1646.36	1646.36	1646.36	1646.36
O-6	10,106.70	10,369.20	10,877.70	10,877.70	11,094.90	11,094.90	11,094.90	11,094.90	11,094.90	11,094.90
1 Drill	336.89	345.64	362.59	362.59	369.83	369.83	369.83	369.83	369.83	369.83
4 Drills	1,347.56	1,382.56	1,450.36	1,450.36	1,479.32	1,479.32	1,479.32	1,479.32	1,479.32	1,479.32
O-5	8,876.40	8,876.40	8,876.40	8,876.40	8,876.40	8,876.40	8,876.40	8,876.40	8,876.40	8,876.40
1 Drill	295.88	295.88	295.88	295.88	295.88	295.88	295.88	295.88	295.88	295.88
4 Drills	1,183.52	1,183.52	1,183.52	1,183.52	1,183.52	1,183.52	1,183.52	1,183.52	1,183.52	1,183.52
O-4	7,526.70	7,526.70	7,526.70	7,526.70	7,526.70	7,526.70	7,526.70	7,526.70	7,526.70	7,526.70
1 Drill	250.89	250.89	250.89	250.89	250.89	250.89	250.89	250.89	250.89	250.89
4 Drills	1,003.56	1,003.56	1,003.56	1,003.56	1,003.56	1,003.56	1,003.56	1,003.56	1,003.56	1,003.56
O-3	6,448.20	6,448.20	6,448.20	6,448.20	6,448.20	6,448.20	6,448.20	6,448.20	6,448.20	6,448.20
1 Drill	214.94	214.94	214.94	214.94	214.94	214.94	214.94	214.94	214.94	214.94
4 Drills	859.76	859.76	859.76	859.76	859.76	859.76	859.76	859.76	859.76	859.76
O-2	4,739.40	4,739.40	4,739.40	4,739.40	4,739.40	4,739.40	4,739.40	4,739.40	4,739.40	4,739.40
1 Drill	157.98	157.98	157.98	157.98	157.98	157.98	157.98	157.98	157.98	157.98
4 Drills	631.92	631.92	631.92	631.92	631.92	631.92	631.92	631.92	631.92	631.92
O-1	3,740.10	3,740.10	3,740.10	3,740.10	3,740.10	3,740.10	3,740.10	3,740.10	3,740.10	3,740.10
1 Drill	124.67	124.67	124.67	124.67	124.67	124.67	124.67	124.67	124.67	124.67
4 Drills	498.68	498.68	498.68	498.68	498.68	498.68	498.68	498.68	498.68	498.68
O-3E	6,881.40	6,881.40	6,881.40	6,881.40	6,881.40	6,881.40	6,881.40	6,881.40	6,881.40	6,881.40
1 Drill	229.38	229.38	229.38	229.38	229.38	229.38	229.38	229.38	229.38	229.38
4 Drills	917.52	917.52	917.52	917.52	917.52	917.52	917.52	917.52	917.52	917.52
O-2E	5,488.50	5,488.50	5,488.50	5,488.50	5,488.50	5,488.50	5,488.50	5,488.50	5,488.50	5,488.50
1 Drill	182.95	182.95	182.95	182.95	182.95	182.95	182.95	182.95	182.95	182.95
4 Drills	731.80	731.80	731.80	731.80	731.80	731.80	731.80	731.80	731.80	731.80
O-1E	4,643.70	4,643.70	4,643.70	4,643.70	4,643.70	4,643.70	4,643.70	4,643.70	4,643.70	4,643.70
1 Drill	154.79	154.79	154.79	154.79	154.79	154.79	154.79	154.79	154.79	154.79
4 Drills	619.16	619.16	619.16	619.16	619.16	619.16	619.16	619.16	619.16	619.16

DRILL PAY—EFFECTIVE JANUARY 1, 2016

Pay Grade	2 or less	Over 2	Over 3	Over 4	Over 6	Over 8	Over 10	Over 12	Over 14	Over 16	Over 18	Over 20
W-5												7,283.10
1 Drill												242.77
4 Drills												971.08
W-4	4,095.90	4,406.10	4,532.40	4,656.90	4,871.10	5,083.20	5,298.00	5,620.80	5,904.00	6,173.40	6,393.90	6,608.70
1 Drill	136.53	146.87	151.08	155.23	162.37	169.44	176.60	187.36	196.80	205.78	213.13	220.29
4 Drills	546.12	587.48	604.32	620.92	649.48	677.76	706.40	749.44	787.20	823.12	852.52	881.16
W-3	3,740.40	3,896.40	4,056.30	4,108.80	4,276.20	4,605.90	4,949.10	5,110.80	5,297.70	5,490.30	5,836.50	6,070.50
1 Drill	124.68	129.88	135.21	136.96	142.54	153.53	164.97	170.36	176.59	183.01	194.55	202.35
4 Drills	498.72	519.52	540.84	547.84	570.16	614.12	659.88	681.44	706.36	732.04	778.20	809.40
W-2	3,309.90	3,622.80	3,719.40	3,785.40	4,000.20	4,333.80	4,499.10	4,661.70	4,860.90	5,016.30	5,157.30	5,325.90
1 Drill	110.33	120.76	123.98	126.18	133.34	144.46	149.97	155.39	162.03	167.21	171.91	177.53
4 Drills	441.32	483.04	495.92	504.72	533.36	577.84	599.88	621.56	648.12	668.84	687.64	710.12
W-1	2,905.50	3,218.10	3,302.10	3,479.70	3,690.00	3,999.60	4,144.20	4,346.10	4,545.00	4,701.60	4,845.30	5,020.50
1 Drill	96.85	107.27	110.07	115.99	123.00	133.32	138.14	144.87	151.50	156.72	161.51	167.35
4 Drills	387.40	429.08	440.28	463.96	492.00	533.28	552.56	579.48	606.00	626.88	646.04	669.40

Pay Grade	Over 22	Over 24	Over 26	Over 28	Over 30	Over 32	Over 34	Over 36	Over 38	Over 40
W-5	7,652.40	7,927.50	8,232.30	8,232.30	8,644.50	8,644.50	9,076.20	9,076.20	9,530.70	9,530.70
1 Drill	255.08	264.25	274.41	274.41	288.15	288.15	302.54	302.54	317.69	317.69
4 Drills	1,020.32	1,057.00	1,097.64	1,097.64	1,152.60	1,152.60	1,210.16	1,210.16	1,270.76	1,270.76
W-4	6,924.60	7,184.10	7,480.20	7,480.20	7,629.60	7,629.60	7,629.60	7,629.60	7,629.60	7,629.60
1 Drill	230.82	239.47	249.34	249.34	254.32	254.32	254.32	254.32	254.32	254.32
4 Drills	923.28	957.88	997.36	997.36	1,017.28	1,017.28	1,017.28	1,017.28	1,017.28	1,017.28
W-3	6,210.30	6,359.10	6,561.60	6,561.60	6,561.60	6,561.60	6,561.60	6,561.60	6,561.60	6,561.60
1 Drill	207.01	211.97	218.72	218.72	218.72	218.72	218.72	218.72	218.72	218.72
4 Drills	828.04	847.88	874.88	874.88	874.88	874.88	874.88	874.88	874.88	874.88
W-2	5,436.60	5,524.50	5,524.50	5,524.50	5,524.50	5,524.50	5,524.50	5,524.50	5,524.50	5,524.50
1 Drill	181.22	184.15	184.15	184.15	184.15	184.15	184.15	184.15	184.15	184.15
4 Drills	724.88	736.60	736.60	736.60	736.60	736.60	736.60	736.60	736.60	736.60
W-1	5,020.50	5,020.50	5,020.50	5,020.50	5,020.50	5,020.50	5,020.50	5,020.50	5,020.50	5,020.50
1 Drill	167.35	167.35	167.35	167.35	167.35	167.35	167.35	167.35	167.35	167.35
4 Drills	669.40	669.40	669.40	669.40	669.40	669.40	669.40	669.40	669.40	669.40

DRILL PAY—EFFECTIVE JANUARY 1, 2016

Cumulative Years of Service

Grade	2 or less	Over 2	Over 3	Over 4	Over 6	Over 8	Over 10	Over 12	Over 14	Over 16	Over 18	Over 20
E-9							4,948.80	5,060.70	5,202.30	5,368.20	5,536.20	5,804.70
1 Drill							164.96	168.69	173.41	178.94	184.54	193.49
4 Drills							659.84	674.76	693.64	715.76	738.16	773.96
E-8						4,050.90	4,230.00	4,341.00	4,473.90	4,618.20	4,878.00	5,009.40
1 Drill						135.03	141.00	144.70	149.13	153.94	162.60	166.98
4 Drills						540.12	564.00	578.80	596.52	615.76	650.40	667.92
E-7	2,816.10	3,073.50	3,191.40	3,347.10	3,468.90	3,678.00	3,795.60	4,004.70	4,178.70	4,297.50	4,423.80	4,472.70
1 Drill	93.87	102.45	106.38	111.57	115.63	122.60	126.52	133.49	139.29	143.25	147.46	149.09
4 Drills	375.48	409.80	425.52	446.28	462.52	490.40	506.08	533.96	557.16	573.00	589.84	596.36
E-6	2,435.70	2,680.20	2,798.40	2,913.60	3,033.60	3,303.30	3,408.60	3,612.30	3,674.40	3,719.70	3,772.50	3,772.50
1 Drill	81.19	89.34	93.28	97.12	101.12	110.11	113.62	120.41	122.48	123.99	125.75	125.75
4 Drills	324.76	357.36	373.12	388.48	404.48	440.44	454.48	481.64	489.92	495.96	503.00	503.00
E-5	2,231.40	2,381.40	2,496.60	2,614.20	2,797.80	2,989.80	3,147.60	3,166.20	3,166.20	3,166.20	3,166.20	3,166.20
1 Drill	74.38	79.38	83.22	87.14	93.26	99.66	104.92	105.54	105.54	105.54	105.54	105.54
4 Drills	297.52	317.52	332.88	348.56	373.04	398.64	419.68	422.16	422.16	422.16	422.16	422.16
E-4	2,046.00	2,150.40	2,267.10	2,382.00	2,483.40	2,483.40	2,483.40	2,483.40	2,483.40	2,483.40	2,483.40	2,483.40
1 Drill	68.20	71.68	75.57	79.40	82.78	82.78	82.78	82.78	82.78	82.78	82.78	82.78
4 Drills	272.80	286.72	302.28	317.60	331.12	331.12	331.12	331.12	331.12	331.12	331.12	331.12
E-3	1,847.10	1,963.20	2,082.00	2,082.00	2,082.00	2,082.00	2,082.00	2,082.00	2,082.00	2,082.00	2,082.00	2,082.00
1 Drill	61.57	65.44	69.40	69.40	69.40	69.40	69.40	69.40	69.40	69.40	69.40	69.40
4 Drills	246.28	261.76	277.60	277.60	277.60	277.60	277.60	277.60	277.60	277.60	277.60	277.60
E-2	1,756.50	1,756.50	1,756.50	1,756.50	1,756.50	1,756.50	1,756.50	1,756.50	1,756.50	1,756.50	1,756.50	1,756.50
1 Drill	58.55	58.55	58.55	58.55	58.55	58.55	58.55	58.55	58.55	58.55	58.55	58.55
4 Drills	234.20	234.20	234.20	234.20	234.20	234.20	234.20	234.20	234.20	234.20	234.20	234.20
E-1 > 4 mos	1,566.90											
1 Drill	52.23											
4 Drills	208.92											
E-1 < 4 mos	1,449.00											
1 Drill	48.30											
4 Drills	193.20											

DRILL PAY—EFFECTIVE JANUARY 1, 2016

Cumulative Years of Service

Grade	Over 22	Over 24	Over 26	Over 28	Over 30	Over 32	Over 34	Over 36	Over 38	Over 40
E-9	6,032.10	6,270.90	6,636.90	6,636.90	6,968.40	6,968.40	7,317.00	7,317.00	7,683.30	7,683.30
1 Drill	201.07	209.03	221.23	221.23	232.28	232.28	243.90	243.90	256.11	256.11
4 Drills	804.28	836.12	884.92	884.92	929.12	929.12	975.60	975.60	1,024.44	1,024.44
E-8	5,233.80	5,358.00	5,664.00	5,664.00	5,777.70	5,777.70	5,777.70	5,777.70	5,777.70	5,777.70
1 Drill	174.46	178.60	188.80	188.80	192.59	192.59	192.59	192.59	192.59	192.59
4 Drills	697.84	714.40	755.20	755.20	770.36	770.36	770.36	770.36	770.36	770.36
E-7	4,637.10	4,725.30	5,061.30	5,061.30	5,061.30	5,061.30	5,061.30	5,061.30	5,061.30	5,061.30
1 Drill	154.57	157.51	168.71	168.71	168.71	168.71	168.71	168.71	168.71	168.71
4 Drills	618.28	630.04	674.84	674.84	674.84	674.84	674.84	674.84	674.84	674.84
E-6	3,772.50	3,772.50	3,772.50	3,772.50	3,772.50	3,772.50	3,772.50	3,772.50	3,772.50	3,772.50
1 Drill	125.75	125.75	125.75	125.75	125.75	125.75	125.75	125.75	125.75	125.75
4 Drills	503.00	503.00	503.00	503.00	503.00	503.00	503.00	503.00	503.00	503.00
E-5	3,166.20	3,166.20	3,166.20	3,166.20	3,166.20	3,166.20	3,166.20	3,166.20	3,166.20	3,166.20
1 Drill	105.54	105.54	105.54	105.54	105.54	105.54	105.54	105.54	105.54	105.54
4 Drills	422.16	422.16	422.16	422.16	422.16	422.16	422.16	422.16	422.16	422.16
E-4	2,483.40	2,483.40	2,483.40	2,483.40	2,483.40	2,483.40	2,483.40	2,483.40	2,483.40	2,483.40
1 Drill	82.78	82.78	82.78	82.78	82.78	82.78	82.78	82.78	82.78	82.78
4 Drills	331.12	331.12	331.12	331.12	331.12	331.12	331.12	331.12	331.12	331.12
E-3	2,082.00	2,082.00	2,082.00	2,082.00	2,082.00	2,082.00	2,082.00	2,082.00	2,082.00	2,082.00
1 Drill	69.40	69.40	69.40	69.40	69.40	69.40	69.40	69.40	69.40	69.40
4 Drills	277.60	277.60	277.60	277.60	277.60	277.60	277.60	277.60	277.60	277.60
E-2	1,756.50	1,756.50	1,756.50	1,756.50	1,756.50	1,756.50	1,756.50	1,756.50	1,756.50	1,756.50
1 Drill	58.55	58.55	58.55	58.55	58.55	58.55	58.55	58.55	58.55	58.55
4 Drills	234.20	234.20	234.20	234.20	234.20	234.20	234.20	234.20	234.20	234.20

commanders may have more flexibility than they do now to hand out merit-based cash bonuses to individual troops.

Today's one-size-fits-all pay chart could ultimately become a relic for the history books. Is that a good thing or a bad thing? No one knows for sure. Time will tell.

Beyond Base Pay: Allowances, Special Pay, and Bonuses

The Congressional Budget Office (CBO) reportedly estimated that the average active duty service member receives benefits and pay compensation packages worth $99,000, which sounds like so much, doesn't it?

If you look at your spouse's last LES and wonder how that can possibly be, consider that base pay does not include the often tax-exempt bonuses, allowances, and other potential benefits that make up a significant piece of a total compensation package.

See figure 2.1 for 2016 rates of allowence and incentive and special pays.

BASIC ALLOWANCE FOR HOUSING (BAH) AND OVERSEAS HOUSING ALLOWANCE (OHA)

BAH is a U.S. base allowance that provides uniformed service members equitable housing compensation based on housing costs in local markets when government quarters are not provided.

Those who are stationed overseas who do not live in government housing may be eligible for Overseas Housing Allowance (OHA). If you are stationed somewhere that the dollar-to-host-nation currency is less than equitable, you will come to greatly appreciate this allowance if you don't already.

BAH/OHA are important allowances, particularly for younger couples and families who may be stationed in high-cost-of-living areas. These generous amounts, however, are not designed to cover all housing costs for all service members. If you happen to live on the military installation in government housing, you don't receive it.

BAH/OHA rates are based on local rent costs and vary by location, pay grade, and dependency status. The cost of utilities and renters' insurance is also considered. A rate protection is also included so that service members who have made long-term contractual housing commitments are not penalized in the event of a decrease in the rate change. To figure out your BAH/OHA rate, visit www.defensetravel.dod.mil.

BASIC ALLOWANCE FOR SUBSISTENCE (BAS)

Not only do you potentially receive funds to offset your rent or mortgage, but you also receive funds to help put food on the table. BAS is a nontaxable amount that is designed to offset the cost of service member meals.

In 2016, the monthly BAS rate for enlisted service members was $368.29 and $253.63 for officers.

DISLOCATION ALLOWANCE (DLA)

Moving is an expensive fact of life in the military. The DLA helps to make it a little less financially challenging. DLA is used to partially reimburse a service member who has or doesn't have family members for expenses not otherwise reimbursed that are incurred during a PCS move, a move ordered for the convenience of the government, or because of an evacuation.

DLA is a considered an additional allowance and may even be paid in advance, which can be quite convenient when you are facing a move. Like other allowances, however, it doesn't cover *all* relocation expenses, so don't expect it to do so.

National Guard and Reserve members who are coming on or leaving active duty are not eligible for DLA unless coming on active duty for more than twenty weeks at one location and authorized PCS allowances in the first place.

Sometimes in military life, you have to move for other reasons beyond mission requirements. For example, say you live in government quarters and the government wants to renovate or privatize them. In those cases, and in others, a partial DLA may be paid to the service member who is ordered to leave government quarters because of those types of reasons.

DLA rate information can be found on the DoD Per Diem, Travel and Transportation Allowance Committee DLA website, http://www .defensetravel.dod.mil/site/allowances.cfm.

FAMILY SEPARATION ALLOWANCE (FSA)

If your service member has to serve on an unaccompanied tour (meaning you don't get to go), then he or she may be entitled to a family separation allowance of $250 per month.

If you are entitled to move along with your uniformed spouse and you choose not to do so, then you do not get this allowance. This happens more than you might imagine, too. *Geobaching* is becoming more common with military families, particularly for those spouses who have good jobs and don't want to give them up when permanent change of station (PCS) orders arrive.

To learn more about FSA, visit http://militarypay.defense.gov/PAY/ALLOWANCES/FSA.ASPX.

There are also potential allowances available to eligible families who may be struggling financially to make ends meet.

FAMILY SUBSISTENCE SUPPLEMENTAL ALLOWANCE (FSSA)

FSSA is a voluntary financial benefits program for military families intended to increase a service member's income in order to remove their household from eligibility for Supplemental Nutrition Assistance Program (SNAP) benefits (formerly the food stamp program).

For more information, visit http://www.dmdc.osd.mil/fssa/, or pay a visit to the financial readiness program at the family center on the nearest military installation.

WOMEN, INFANTS AND CHILDREN (WIC)

WIC is a food and nutrition program established in 1974 and funded by the U.S. Department of Agriculture. It provides families with funding for nutritious food, tips on how to prepare balanced meals, nutrition and health screenings, and other resources. You can learn more about WIC in the United States at http://www.fns.usda.gov/wic/who-gets-wic-and-how-apply and WIC Overseas at http://www.tricare.mil/Plans/SpecialPrograms/WICOverseas.aspx.

In addition to all of the above, the DoD also pays to dress your service member in those dashing military uniforms.

MILITARY CLOTHING ALLOWANCE

Any die-hard shopper knows clothes can be expensive. Military uniforms may not be designer in nature, but the price for multiple sets with the requisite patches and insignia bling can add up quickly.

Lucky for you, initial, replacement, maintenance, and extra clothing allowances may be issued to help service members pay for their uniforms.

Both officers and enlisted members are entitled to an initial clothing allowance.

Enlisted service members may receive it initially and then annually to cover wear-and-tear costs. They also may receive this allowance once they obtain special qualifications. After three years of active service, they may also receive a maintenance allowance to fund the replacement of items.

Officers, however, are only entitled to this initial allowance once except in unique circumstances.

Those whose job requires civilian clothes rather than military uniforms while on duty are also able to receive an extra clothing allowance for civilian attire.

SPECIAL AND INCENTIVE PAYS

The DoD pays service members a little something extra for having a unique skill set or for doing an especially difficult job. These monies are called *special and incentive pay* and they vary by pay grade and years in service.

Examples of special and incentive pays include Hardship Duty Pay (HDP), Hostile Fire Pay/Imminent Danger Pay (HFP/IDP), Assignment Incentive Pay (AIP), and Hazardous Duty Incentive Pay (HDIP).

Special and incentive pays are often tax exempt, and receipt of them can help you and your spouse increase your savings.

There is an unfortunate catch here, however. To earn such types of pay, your spouse must be working and living in harm's way in an environment where bullets may be flying over his head.

UNDERSTANDING THE LEAVE AND EARNINGS STATEMENT (LES)

You might be confused the first time you look at an LES, as there is a lot of information crammed into one form and often in tiny print.

The Leave and Earnings Statement (LES), though, is important to understand. It is a comprehensive statement showing a service member's total pay and leave days for a specific pay period. It can be accessed online through one's myPay account 24/7. Each branch of service has its own version of the LES, but they all basically contain the same type of information.

The LES form includes personal service member data to include name, Social Security number, pay grade, pay date, years of service, expiration of term of service date (ETS), branch of service, identifying number of disbursing office, and pay period covered.

The LES also includes information regarding the service member's entitlements, deductions, and allotments. It shows the date one entered the military, the associated retirement plan, and the balances of earned and used leave amounts.

Additionally, the LES provides tax information such as amount of federal tax withheld, FICA, state tax, and any additional pay data. It also details the amounts saved in the service member's Thrift Savings Plan (TSP).

Timeless LES Tips

Always review the LES. Make sure the numbers add up and the right deductions and allowances are being made.

For example, is the stated base pay correct? If you're not sure, look it up on the current pay chart included in this chapter or on the DFAS site at http://www.dfas.mil/militarymembers/payentitlements/military-pay-charts.html.

Is your service member receiving the correct amount of BAH/OHA? To clarify your BAH/OHA rates, visit the Defense Travel Management Office website at http://www.defensetravel.dod.mil. Click on the Programs and Services and then on Allowances tab. You can either review rates for all stateside and overseas locations or you can plug in a specific zip code and find out an exact rate quickly.

Monitor the leave balance. Service members earn 2.5 days per month. Leave accumulated over seventy-five days can be lost, so you want to watch those numbers and take a vacation before you lose those days.

If you find an error on the LES, take steps to resolve it immediately. Correcting pay-related errors can be time consuming and painful, particularly if you were overpaid for some reason. Service members can visit their finance office or administrative section for assistance, or they can access the myPay Assistance and Customer Support option on the DFAS myPay website.

KNOW YOUR IMPORTANT MILITARY BENEFITS

In addition to base pay, allowances, and special and incentive pays, there are a number of valuable benefits available to service members and their families that you should become familiar with in order to take advantage of them while you are in the greater military family, and, in some cases, later, when you leave it behind.

Military Retirement Plan

As a new military family, the thought of your service member retiring after twenty years may seem way too far in the future to contemplate. You'd be surprised at how quickly the time can fly.

Of course, the majority of those who serve transition out of uniform before reaching retirement eligibility at twenty years of service. Still, it could happen to you, and here's what you should know for now.

The existing retirement plan is a good deal. The day your service member retires from the military, he or she starts collecting a regular retirement pension. If someone enters the military at eighteen and retires twenty years later, then at thirty-eight years old he could be receiving a decent monthly pension check.

There are, of course, a number of factors that determine exactly how much of a pension someone will earn, such as the date of entry into service.

Essentially, however, if someone serves for twenty years, he is eligible to receive a pension based on a percentage of base pay. If he manages to stay in for a whopping forty years, he is eligible for 100 percent of his base pay.

You should also know that this good deal will not last. How retirements are handled for future service members and even perhaps for some current ones will be significantly changed.

In November 2015, President Obama signed a budget and policy bill, turning the 2016 annual defense authorization bill into law. As a result, the traditional military retirement system that has been revered for decades will be transformed into a blended pension and investment system that includes automatic contributions to troops' Thrift Savings Plans and the opportunity for government matches to personal contributions.[5]

The new retirement system is anticipated to shrink the size of the current pension by about 20 percent while giving four in five service members who leave the military some sort of retirement benefit where it currently only pays out for one in five now.

Those who retire from the military with this new plan could see much smaller monthly retirement paychecks while they are of working age. Once they reach age sixty, however, that money and potentially more could be restored to the service member.

Those who are already serving in uniform may have a choice of which retirement program they wish to fall under, but those who enter military service on or after January 1, 2018, certainly won't.

While retirement may not seem like a timely topic to you at this stage of your life, it should be. You will eventually want (or need) to retire, and you will want to have the funds available to do so. No one, repeat no one, cares as much about your future well-being as you do. While you have the luxury of time to grow your nest egg, do it.

You can keep current on all the changes at http://www.dfas.mil/retiredmilitary/plan/retirement-types.html.

Thrift Savings Plan (TSP)

The TSP is a retirement savings and investment plan for members of the uniformed services, including the Ready Reserve. Federal employees also have the TSP available to them. It is the government's version of a 401(k) plan.

The TSP is a defined contribution plan. To participate in it, service members must have elected a minimum of 1 percent of their base pay for either a traditional or Roth TSP contribution. There are annual contribution limits. Plan participants may change their TSP elections as their life and financial goals change.

To learn more about TSP, visit http://www.dfas.mil/military members/tspformilitary/tspac.html and https://www.tsp.gov/index.shtml.

Use the Thrift Savings Plan (TSP)—even if you're the most junior person in the military. You will have a future afterwards. If you're unsure or even struggling financially, start by contributing $25 per pay period. After six months, make it $50 per payday. Up it a little at a time until you are putting 10 percent of your check per pay period into the TSP and then switch to saving 10 percent rather than a set amount per pay period. When you increase TSP, rank, or the military gets a pay raise, then you will have automatically increased the total amount you're saving without any new effort.

—Kate Numerick, U.S. Army, Dual Serving Family

The DoD Savings Deposit Program (SDP)

If your uniformed spouse is ever deployed to a combat zone and he or she receives tax-exempt Hostile Fire Pay/Imminent Danger Pay (HFP/IDP), then consider taking advantage of the SDP, a special savings account that earns 10 percent interest while your spouse is deployed in a combat zone. Interest earned on the savings is taxable, however. Eligibility for the program stops when your uniformed loved one leaves the combat zone.

For more information about the SDP, visit http://www.dfas.mil/militarymembers/payentitlements/sdp.html.

HEALTH CARE

One of the most valuable benefits your family will appreciate is TRICARE, the military's health care program, which includes medical, dental, and vision. Your uniformed spouse must ensure that eligible family members are enrolled in the DEERS database before being able to use those services.

TRICARE offers a number of different health plans for its beneficiaries to include Prime, Prime Remote, Prime Overseas, Prime Remote Overseas, Standard and Extra, Standard Overseas, TRICARE for Life, Reserve Select, Retired Reserve, Young Adult, and US Family Health Plan.

All TRICARE plans meet or exceed the requirements for minimum essential coverage under the Affordable Care Act.

Plan availability can vary depending on where you happen to be stationed.

TRICARE also offers special programs in areas to include autism, cancer clinical trials, chiropractic health care, combat-related special compensation, computer/electronic accommodations, extended care options, transitional health care, TRICARE Philippine Demonstration, TRICARE Plus, and Women, Infants and Children (WIC) Overseas Program.

TRICARE (http://www.tricare.mil) enrollees (that would be you and any other eligible family members) receive most health care at Military Treatment Facilities (MTF) located on a military installation where you are assigned a primary care manager. MTFs, for clarity's sake, translated into English, are medical clinics. Theoretically, you consistently see your primary care manager when you make appointments.

Sometimes you can't get the services you need at the base or post MTF for any number of possible reasons to include shortage of military health care professionals, patient overload, or the need for specialized care. In those instances and others, TRICARE lets you access a network of "preferred" or "in-network" providers. You are able to freely make your own appointments with authorized providers.

Dental coverage is separate from TRICARE's medical coverage. Active duty service members receive most of their care at military dental clinics. Family members, however, may enroll in the voluntary TRICARE Dental Program.

Dental coverage for Guard and Reserve members is dependent upon the military status at the time the service member is seeking dental care. When not activated, Guard and Reserve families can enroll in the TRICARE Dental Program.

Eligibility to take advantage of TRICARE vision benefits, including eye exams, depends on who you are, your existing TRICARE plan, and your age.

TRICARE also offers services in mental health care, pharmacy, and special needs.

To learn more about TRICARE, visit http://www.tricare.mil.

LIFE INSURANCE

The Veteran's Affairs (VA) Department offers service and eligible family members various options in life insurance. Your service member is automatically covered under Servicemembers Group Life Insurance (SGLI), a program that provides low-cost group life insurance to eligible service members. Premiums cost .07 cents per $1,000 as of 2015, regardless of the member's age. The maximum coverage of SGLI is $400,000.

Service members covered under SGLI are also provided Servicemembers Group Life Insurance Traumatic Injury Protection (TSGLI). TSGLI provides short-term financial assistance to severely injured service members and veterans to help as they recover.

Family Servicemembers Group Life Insurance (FSGLI) is a program that provides term insurance coverage to the spouse and dependent children of service members insured under the SGLI. Spousal coverage costs, while dependent children are insured at no cost. FSGLI provides up to a maximum of $100,000 for spouse, not to exceed the service member's SGLI coverage and $10,000 for dependent children.

When service members separate or retire from the military, they retain SGLI for a short time period only and may then have the option to convert to Veterans Group Life Insurance (VGLI).

For more information on insurance coverage for military service members and their families, visit http://www.benefits.va.gov/INSURANCE/index.asp.

Other VA Benefits

In addition to providing life insurance coverage, the VA provides service members and their families with a host of benefits and services. Many of these benefits become available to service members once they retire and/or transition out of the military. See chapter 8, "Mission Transition" for more information, or review the VA benefit fact sheets at http://benefits.va.gov/BENEFITS/factsheets.asp.

VACATION

Military service members work hard, so they get time to play hard, too. Time off in the military is considered a key element to readiness and well-being. Active duty service members receive thirty days of vacation annually and sick days as needed. Unless the mission demands it, weekends and holidays are often considered free downtime.

Enjoy the thirty-day vacation run now as it rarely exists in the civilian world. It, along with moving frequently (believe that or not), will be among the things you one day miss the most about military life.

ADOPTION REIMBURSEMENT

Families who chose to adopt a child may be eligible for reimbursement of certain expenses associated with the adoption process up to a maximum of $2,000 per child and not to exceed $5,000 per calendar year.

For more information about adoption reimbursement, visit http:// www.dfas.mil/militarymembers/payentitlements/adoptionreimbursement. html.

Space-A Travel

Another cool perk is Space-A Travel on military flights. The *A* stands for *available*, meaning if there is space available, then service members, retirees, certain DoD employees, and eligible family members can fly for free unless you are traveling internationally, in which case you may have to pay a small departure tax.

Space-A sounds great, and it can be if you are prepared to be flexible on your dates of travel and willing to adjust your plans if need be on a moment's notice. Military flights can be delayed or cancelled unexpectedly, and you aren't able to reserve a seat. You show up to the military passenger terminal (airport) with the right paperwork in hand, sign in, and wait.

Eligible family members may travel without their active duty sponsor when that sponsor is deployed for more than 120 days.

There is a lot of fine print you need to know about if you want to fly Space-A. You can learn all about it at http://www.amc.af.mil/amctravel/ index.asp.

Benefits are subject to change over time, so keep up with those changes that could directly affect you and your family, positively or negatively. Those military benefits are important, and when you add the value of those items to your base pay, you can kind of see where the Congressional Budget Office came up with the numbers.

Live life, but please please, please, do not forget to SAVE! You never know if you will get out after your first term.

—Nat Benipayo, U.S. Air Force Spouse (Retired)

MILITARY MONEY MANAGEMENT BASICS

Stop buying brand-new cars that are too expensive for your paycheck.

—Debbie Milby, U.S. Army (Retired) and U.S. Army Spouse

Understanding the numbers on an LES is one thing. Effectively managing them can be another challenge altogether. There are many obstacles, seen and unseen, that can prevent you from reaching your financial goals.

If you haven't quite figured it out yet, the military lifestyle can be a highly unpredictable one. You don't always know what's going to happen, when it's going to happen, and what costly out-of-pocket expenses you may have in the process.

Sometimes you do know what is going to happen and it still punches you in the wallet. For example, let's say you are a family who is accustomed to having two paychecks, yours and the one Uncle Sam pays the uniformed love of your life. When PCS orders arrive telling you to pack up and move to your next home, one paycheck may disappear until you are settled down again and find a new job. If you are relocating to an area with poor employment prospects, you could be looking at a whole new reality.

Unless you have a great job and decide to stay put while your spouse moves on, job loss, job search, and paycheck interruptus are military lifestyle facts of life.

While you can't always predict what will come your way, you and your spouse can work together to manage your finances as effectively as possible.

Of course, working together on all things money, even with someone you love, can be an obstacle in and of itself on occasion, particularly if you view money management through different lenses.

Perhaps you have a knack for saving a buck and he sees nothing wrong with maxing out every credit card. Or you practice retail therapy to a fault in order to cope with military life stressors and he forgets to tell you about ATM withdrawals. Everyone has his or her own money personality. It's not uncommon for those personalities to clash, and the financial results can be disastrous on many levels, both within the military world and outside of it.

If you and your spouse can't seem to see eye to eye on how to manage the family finances together, admit it and get outside assistance on the matter. Visit the military family center's financial readiness program and take advantage of the many classes and financial counseling possibilities there.

Creating a Livable Spending Plan and Sticking to It

At the heart of financial readiness, you'll find a carefully crafted spending plan. A spending plan allows you to gain and maintain control over your income and expenses. It doesn't have to be a perfect document that details each item to the penny. It, much like a resume, can be a living, breathing document that adjusts as your circumstances do.

The experts at the financial readiness program at the local family services support center can help you. Even your own personal bank may offer more than just banking. Military-friendly banks, such as USAA, Navy Federal Credit Union, and other similar institutions, are often treasure troves of financial education, knowledge, and genuine support on many levels.

SaveandInvest.org is another good source to help you up your financial literacy game, too.

SaveandInvest.org is a project of the FINRA Investor Education Foundation that offers free and unbiased resources to military personnel through a DoD Memorandum of Understanding.

They offer the following steps to help you create your own spending plan:

Step 1: *Add up your monthly expenses.* Include such items as your mortgage or rent, car payment, insurance premiums, utilities, and phone bills.

Step 2: *Add up your monthly take-home (after tax) pay for you and your spouse.* Include any additional investment or rental income.

Step 3: *Subtract the monthly expenses from the monthly income amount and analyze the results.* If your resulting number is zero or below, figure out where you can cut expenses.

You need to be able to pay those bills you have to pay. If you can't, then consider how you can eliminate or cut back on the flexible expenses. You might also consider how you could earn more by creating a new income stream.

Meeting the day-to-day basics is important, but you also need to look toward your future, too. What are your financial goals, and how can you reach them? Maybe you want to establish an emergency fund, become debt-free, or pay for college.

You can do that with thoughtful planning. Simply estimate the cost for each goal and when you'd like to have that goal met. Divide the time (in months) into this amount, and you will have a monthly savings target for each goal.

Don't be scared to adjust your expenses and goals along the way. Make a date with yourself to review your spending plan and financial goals every payday when you also pay your bills.

Setting aside dedicated time to pay your bills and manage your money may be time consuming at first, but eventually you will be on maintenance mode. The goal here is to effectively manage your money so that it doesn't manage you.

> Be wise with your money and always have a decent-sized savings account.
>
> —Pam Cabana Macken, U.S. Air Spouse (Retired) and
> U.S. Air Force Brat

Military Family Home Front Savings Strategies

Big or small, the following strategies can help you whether you are saving for a new or quality used car, a down payment on a house, or you simply want to grow your long-term savings.

- *Routinely save your small change in a jar.* When it is full, wrap the coins and deposit them.
- *Bring your lunch to work.* Buying lunch out every day can be expensive. Instead, pack leftovers from weeknight dinners.
- *Use coupons.* Take advantage of any military-specific discounts that you may be eligible to use. Deposit your "savings" toward one of your financial goals. If you are stationed overseas, coupons may be used past their stated expiration date for six months in some locations. Ask at the local commissary.
- *Shop on the military installation.* While we still have them, use the commissaries and post or base exchanges. Don't forget to use those coupons there, too.
- *Shop wisely.* Research and compare the cost of items, particularly high-end items that are expensive, *before* you buy them so you can select the better deal.
- Buy nonperishable food items in bulk, but only if you are truly going to use them.

Financial Readiness Smart Strategies

Most financial experts will agree that these beautifully basic strategies can serve as a solid foundation to financial readiness:

- Don't spend more than you earn. Learn to live within your means.
- Pay your bills on time, all the time.

- If you have existing debt, don't create any new debt and work consistently to pay off any outstanding balances.
- Start an emergency or rainy-day fund because into your life rain will certainly fall at some point. Even small amounts eventually add up if you let them.
- Once debt is paid off, focus on long-term savings.
- Balance your spending and savings efforts realistically. It makes no sense to save a large sum of money in long-term savings each month if you are racking up daily charges to make ends meet.
- Get and/or maintain good credit.
- Protect your credit. Read "Your Good Credit: Maintaining and Protecting It" later in this chapter to help you.
- Anticipate events that could cause a change in your cash flow, such as a permanent change of station (PCS) move, and prepare for it financially before it occurs.
- Organize your financial information. Using a simple spreadsheet, you can easily keep track of account numbers, websites, and log-ins for your bank accounts, loans, credit cards, investments, and insurance policies. Also note the location of important documents such as your wills, power of attorney, birth certificates, marriage certificate(s), and other legal documents. Keep your "executive summary" in a safe location such as a safe deposit box, and make sure at least one other person you trust can access it if need be.
- Monitor your finances routinely to make sure you get on track and stay on track.

Spend wisely. There are no Joneses that you have to keep up with here.

—Aubrey Kaufman, DoD Civilian Employee

Military Family Finance Goal: Become Debt Free

Debt free is the way to be. Say it loud and say it proud. Getting to that point, however, can be frustrating, but it can be done. Staying there can be challenging at times, too.

Here are some tips to help you get there and stay there:

Stop creating new debt. From this moment forward, you pay with cash or you don't buy whatever it is that calls to you.

Design a livable spending plan. Any extra money you have should then be applied toward your debt.

Consider debt consolidation if it makes sense. Combine your debts into one low-interest loan. Be sure you compare loan interest rates first, however. Also, don't fool yourself into thinking you have *only* one debt afterward and start racking up new debt. If you want to truly be out of debt, you have to think differently than you have before.

Suck it up and pay it all off step by step. Pay off your debts by first making a list of them that includes the creditor's name, total amount owed, the interest rate, and the minimum balance due monthly. Then, take another look at your spending plan. (If you don't have one, create one first.)

Allocate any leftover cash monthly to the highest-interest debt while continuing to pay the minimum on the others. Once the first debt is paid off, use the money you used to pay it and apply it along with the minimum to the debt with the next-highest rate. Pay. Pay off. Repeat this process until all your debt is gone.

Alternatively, you could also start the process by paying off the smallest debt first, regardless of the interest rate.

If you are unable to pay your bills, don't hide from reality, as doing so will only make matters worse. Instead, call your creditors. Explain your situation and ask them if they can work with you to develop an affordable payment plan. If they are willing and able, be sure you get it in writing just in case you need to substantiate your efforts at some point.

Once you have paid off your debt, don't backslide. Credit is a tool and you should be able to use it wisely. Going forward, don't charge more than you can pay off within the month. Or, don't charge at all.

If you are struggling financially or if you want to learn more about personal financial management, to include savings and investing strategies, consult with a financial readiness counselor at the military family center.

Make a genuine effort to be financially literate. Education is key to your future success, and the military family center financial readiness program experts can provide that to you at no charge. You don't have to do much research to figure out the price is right there.

Don't spend beyond your means.

—Anonymous Military Spouse

YOUR GOOD CREDIT:
MAINTAINING AND PROTECTING IT

Your credit, as you might strongly suspect, is important to your financial well-being. Without good credit, lenders may not lend you money to buy a car or a house. Or if they do, they will tack on a higher interest rate in the process. Insurers may decide against insuring you. Employers may not hire you. Property managers may not rent to you if you have a bad history of paying your bills.

It may help you to think of your credit report as a report card. It tells others how responsible you are when it comes to handling your money and suggests how responsible you may be handling the money of others who lend theirs to you.

What does your current report card say about you? Do you play well with others? Are you a delight to have in the classroom of life? Are there some areas you can improve upon?

To find out the answers to these kinds of questions, you have to review your credit report. There are three credit bureaus in the United States, and they are listed below along with their web address and toll-free telephone number:

- *Equifax*, http://www.equifax.com, 1-800-525-6285
- *Experian*, http://www.experian.com, 1-888-397-3742
- *TransUnion*, http://www.transunion.com, 1-800-680-7289

You can request a copy of your credit report from any of the three at any time for a small fee; however, you are entitled to a *free* copy of your credit report from each bureau each year.

To request your free reports from each of the credit bureaus, visit the website www.annualcreditreport.com. Make sure you use that particular web address, as there are many look-alike sites out there that charge you for the reports.

Really Understanding Your Credit Report

It is important to carefully read your credit reports when you receive them.

At first glance, the report may seem overwhelming, but you have to take a deep breath and read it line by line. Each one of the reports may be different because those who do the reporting on your credit activity don't always report to the same bureau.

At a bare minimum, you should understand what is on your credit report, what your credit score is, and how to correct any errors should you find any.

What Shows Up on Your Credit Report

- Your name, address, Social Security number, and date of birth. It may also include employment information.
- Information about your existing credit card accounts, mortgages, car loans, and student loans. It may also reveal account balances owed, terms of loan agreements, and how good (or not) you have been about making payments.
- Public record details. For example, if you have filed for bankruptcy, had any court judgments made against you, or have any tax liens against your property, those will appear on your credit report.
- If anyone has requested a copy of your credit report, it will be noted.
- There are three main credit bureaus that collect information about your financial doings from your creditors and public records. Each of the bureaus obtains their information about you from different places, so it's important you look at all three of your reports.
- Review your credit report as well as the report for anyone in your immediate family with a Social Security number carefully. Make sure there are no mistakes on it, and make sure you are familiar with every noted institution and/or account number on it.

Commonly Found Mistakes and What to Do About Them

Mistakes happen, and examples of ones commonly found on credit reports include the following:

- Misspelled name, incorrect street address, or a name mixup with someone else.
- Incorrect account details such as an account showing as open when you have closed it or a credit card with the wrong credit limit posted.
- Fake accounts, meaning that someone other than yourself has used your identity.

CORRECTING MISTAKES ON YOUR CREDIT REPORT

If you spot an error on your credit reports, you'll need to contract the credit bureau and let them know about it. You may also need to contact the company that shows up as an error directly.

Also consider adding a security freeze on your credit reports. This will prevent you and anyone pretending to be you from opening any new lines of credit.

What's Your Number? Understanding Your Credit Score

The credit report is only one piece of the credit puzzle. The other piece you need to be concerned about is your credit score if you ever wish to buy a house, a car, or obtain another type of loan.

Would-be lenders use your *credit score* to see if you are creditworthy. Credit scores are developed using the information in your credit report, so you can see why the two pieces are important.

Each of the three credit reporting bureaus has its own credit score, based on the content of your credit report with them. VantageScore and FICO are two others, with FICO being the most widely used score by lenders.

FICO scores are credit scores developed by a company called FICO, formerly known as Fair Isaac Corporation, and they analyze the information on your credit reports and generate a number that supposedly helps lenders predict future behavior based on past behavior.

The scores range from 300 to 850. The higher your score, the better your chances in obtaining favorable rates when you want to borrow money, as you seem less financially risky to lenders or insurers.

Your FICO score is determined by a number of factors that can include your payment history (how well you pay your bills on time), the amount of debt you carry, the age of your credit history, new credit or inquiries, and a mixture of items in your account (the type of credit you have).

You can request your credit report, but that doesn't mean your credit score will be included. Credit scores are not free of charge. That said, before you fork over $20 to purchase your FICO score, pay a visit to the financial readiness program at your local military family center. You may be able to get it completely free of charge on the spot thanks to the FINRA Investor Education Program, which has recently made FICO credit scores and analysis tools available free of charge to active duty service members and their spouses.

Be wise with how you spend money. You do not want to completely deprive yourself, but at the same time, you need to look to the future . . . the planned and UNFORESEEN! And as much as possible, have a decent savings account because you never know when you will need it.

—Heather Unruh, U.S. Air Force Spouse

SCAMS, FRAUD, AND IDENTIFY THEFT

You and your spouse work hard for the money you earn. You work hard to build a good reputation in whatever it is you do professionally.

You need to work hard to protect those things, too. Sometimes, though, even working hard won't keep you from feeling the pain of criminal activity.

In June 2015, the Office of Personnel Management (OPM) [the federal government's human resources office] reported being the victim of the largest breach of government data in U.S. history.

Current and former federal employees were affected as well as job applicants (sure to include many military spouses trying to land federal jobs) who were never hired by the federal government. Additionally, anyone, to include active duty service members who applied for an initial security clearance or renewal of a security clearance, may have also been affected.

It's a frustrating situation to say the least.

OPM, however, isn't the only agency to get hit with cybertheft, and it won't be the last, either.

The number of U.S. data breaches in 2015 alone was 781, according to the Identity Theft Resource Center (ITRC). The Federal Trade Commission (FTC) recorded 332,646 identify theft complaints in 2014.

You don't have to look any further than your email's inbox to know that this threat is real.

You can be as vigilant as possible and the bad guys can still get to you one way or another. Even so, don't stop being vigilant, because that could only make a bad situation turn worse.

What to Look Out For

According to the FTC, noticing that you bought a boat, or anything else you didn't really buy yourself, is just one red flag that you might be a victim of identity theft.

There are others.

- You notice mistakes on your bank, credit card, or other account statements.
- There are mistakes on the explanation of medical benefits from your health plan.
- Your regular bills and account statements don't arrive on time, perhaps indicating that someone is intercepting your mail.
- You receive bills or collection notices for products or services you never received and didn't order in the first place.
- The phone starts ringing and debt collectors are on the other end asking you about debts that don't belong to you.
- You receive a notice from the IRS that someone used your Social Security number.
- You receive mail, email, or calls about accounts or jobs in your minor child's name.
- You look over your credit report and see unwarranted collection notices.
- Your personal checks are no good when you try to cash them.
- You thought you nailed the job interview or had a productive conversation with the loan officer at the bank, but you didn't get the job or the loan.

What to Do If You Suspect Foul Play

Place an initial fraud alert on your account. Call any one of three credit reporting agencies (Experian, Equifax, and Transunion) and tell them you are a victim of identity theft and you want an initial fraud alert placed on your credit file.

They should, in turn, call the other two agencies for you and set up alerts there as well. Confirm that they will do this, however.

While you are talking to this credit agency, request a copy of your credit report. It should be free to you as a result of the fraud. You are also eligible by law to receive a free copy of your credit report each year from each of the three agencies.

Order your credit reports from the other two agencies. Call the remaining two credit reporting agencies and tell them you have placed an initial fraud alert on your credit file. They may have been contacted by the first agency already, but if not, they will certainly know now.

Create an identify theft report. Your identity theft report is composed of two parts that include 1) an Identity Theft Affidavit and 2) a police report.

To create the affidavit, you'll have to first notify the FTC about the theft via the Consumer Sentinel–Military or the FTC Complaint Assistant.

File a police report with your local law enforcement agency, on or off post. Be sure to keep copies of everything you submit to anywhere for your own case file.

Once you have notified the FTC and filed a police report, you have created your Identity Theft Report.

Plan to monitor your credit reports, bank accounts, and credit card activity routinely to prevent further damage.

Common Scams Targeted to Military Families

Unfortunately, there are many shady players out there who would love nothing more than to scam military service members and their families out of their hard-earned cash. Scams come in many shapes and sizes. If you're ever wondering whether something is a scam, follow time-tested advice.

If something sounds too good to be true, it probably is.

Below is a short list of commonly employed scams in our military community that you should watch out for and report accordingly if you come across them.

Predatory lending practices are alive, well, and often aimed at young military service members and their families who may not have perfect credit or no credit.

If you are told, No Credit? No Problem, it could be a problem.

The interest rate that a lender offers you in such cases could be astronomical, meaning you end up paying way more for whatever you're buying than it's worth. Sometimes "lenders" will offer to help you get a loan but require you to pay a fee up front.

You pay the fee but you never get the loan.

For-profit colleges with less-than-stellar reputations have jumped on the scam-the-military bandwagon. They will entice service members or eligible family members into using their valuable VA education benefits only to sell them a worthless degree in the long run.

Unscrupulous life insurance agents and so-called financial planners will apply high-pressure sales tactics on service members and their spouses to get them to buy unnecessary and costly insurance policies and financial products.

Another scam involves someone supposedly from the Veterans Affairs (VA) calling service members and telling them that they are updating their personal information and requiring them to tell them theirs for verification purposes.

Military families move around a lot, and that can make them fair game for rental housing scams. Classified ads often target house hunters coming into a new area by offering fake military discounts or by renting a house or apartment to them sight unseen and instructing them to wire required security deposit funds to the landlord.

It should come as no surprise that your Facebook, Twitter, and Instagram accounts are fertile ground for would-be scammers who want to forge close relationships with military service members and families for any number of nefarious reasons.

Always be careful about what you post online. Once it's out there, it's out there. You'll never get it back.

As military family members, we have to be mindful of what we post online even in private group chats among real friends. Not only can we make ourselves easy targets for scammers wanting to take advantage of us financially, but also we can unintentionally jeopardize military readiness and put a lot of people in harm's way by posting seemingly harmless details.

Scammers pretending to be officials from TRICARE send letters to real TRICARE beneficiaries (you) and try to recruit you to be a "Trainee Independent Private Evaluator," aka a secret shopper, for them. They send you a counterfeit TRICARE WPS check for $3,755 and an instruction/ survey form on how to get the check authorized through the company's agent via telephone. You are told to deposit the check at your local bank, retain a percentage of the money, and use the remaining amount to buy six "Vanilla Reload" cards at $500 each at various stores across the country. The "secret shopper" is then told to provide the company agent with the card numbers they bought, complete the survey, and mail it. Once the money has been loaded onto the cards, however, they are immediately available for transfer and the bogus company zeroes out the cards and collects the cash. TRICARE doesn't hire secret shoppers.

Getting Ahead of the Thieves

Use the "active duty alert." If you or your spouse currently serve on active duty and you don't anticipate taking out any new credit, you can place an "active duty alert" on your credit for one year. You can renew it later if you wish to do so. An active duty alert requires creditors to take steps to verify your identity before granting credit in your name.

Review your credit reports routinely. Go to www.annualcreditreport.com or call 877-322-8228 to request your reports. Remember, by law, you are entitled to one free report from each agency each year. Consider purchasing a credit monitoring service from a reputable source such as your bank or credit card company.

Read account statements before you file them away. Make sure your bank, credit card, medical benefit reports, and other account statements reflect accurate charges.

Practice safe surfing. Keep your home and work computers safe from unwanted intrusions by using antivirus and antispyware software. Make sure your firewall is working on your computer, too.

Don't be gullible. Your bank probably doesn't want you to click on a link in an email to confirm your logon and password for them. If you have doubts, don't reply to that email. Instead, pick up the phone and call your bank and talk to them. Or forward that email to your bank to let them know about the scam effort.

Also, pay attention to return email addresses and the grammar and spelling used in messages. Scammers often have a poor command of both.

Protect your digits. Shred documents that have personal information revealed on them. Don't write your Social Security number on your checks or offer up your personal identification numbers anywhere.

Don't overshare. Avoid oversharing your life details on your social network sites. Savvy criminals might be able to figure out the answers to your security questions based on what you reveal to the cyberworld.

Never send money. If someone you've met online asks you to wire him or her money, just don't do it.

> Be flexible. Start saving and investing early and travel as often as possible.
>
> —Shavonne Black-Moore, U.S. Air Force Veteran

ONLINE FINANCIAL RESOURCES

Better Business Bureau, http://www.bbb.org

Consumer Financial Protection Bureau, http://www.consumerfinance.gov

Defense Credit Union Council, http://www.dcuc.org

Defense Finance and Accounting Service, http://www.dfas.mil

Defense Travel Management Office, http://www.defensetravel.dod
.mil/index.cfm

Federal Trade Commission, http://www.consumer.ftc.gov/

Investor Protection Trust, http://www.investorprotection.org

MilitaryMoney.com, http://www.militarymoney.com

MilitaryOneSource.com, http://www.militaryonesource.com

MilitarySaves.org, http://www.militarysaves.org

MyArmyBenefits, http://myarmybenefits.us.army.mil

MyMoney.gov, http://www.mymilitary.gov

MyPay, https://mypay.dfas.mil/mypay.aspx

SaveandInvest.org, http://www.saveandinvest.org

Thrift Savings Plan, https://www.tsp.gov/index.shtml

3

MILITARY FAMILY SUPPORT

Expect not to have your significant other there to help all the time, but there are resources to help if you need them.

—Jessica Leia Moss, U.S. Coast Guard Brat and U.S. Air Force Spouse

Support is something you should never lack as a member of the greater military family. There exists a more-than-robust network of support services available for everyone to include single service members, single parents, young families, empty nesters, those near retirement, and those enjoying their golden years.

Whether you call your installation a *post* like those attached to the Army or a *base* like those from every other service branch, you will find essentially the same type and range of services and programs wherever you happen to be stationed.

Size matters, however. Expect that larger military communities will offer more programs and services than smaller or remote installations.

Of course, support services aren't limited to what is available on the military installation. Your local and global communities, outside the main gate and online, also offer support as well.

I have made some very good friends in the military, and they have helped me to get through some tough times and celebrate the good times.

—Rebecca Roth, U.S. Air Force Spouse

In this chapter, we'll highlight some of the important programs and services you need to be aware of as you launch your military family life journey.

Before we do, however, keep in mind a couple of points.

Throughout your travels in the military, you will notice that each branch of service offers similar programs and services, as was just mentioned above.

You wouldn't always know that, however, by reading the signs.

For example, the sign hanging on the front door of the Army's family center reads *Army Community Service (ACS)*. The sign hanging on the front door of the Navy's family center reads *Fleet and Family Support Center (FFSC)*.

These two different signs say the same thing.

Why should that matter to you if you are a Navy spouse stationed on a Navy base? Good question. While you're there it won't make a bit of difference. When you get stationed on an Army post or within a joint command on an installation where every branch of service is represented, it will be good to know that they are the same thing.

You should also realize that your family member ID card is your passport to all family services, regardless of what type of uniform your sponsor wears wherever you are stationed.

IMPORTANT DOD WEBSITES

Like the saying "there's an app for that," there's also a website for everything, too. You don't have to know all of them, and they certainly aren't all mentioned within the pages of this book. Suffice it to say that information overload is alive and well throughout each branch of service.

The DoD, of course, continues to do its best to figure out how to get the right information out to military families via social media. It's a challenge for them, however, and understandably. Information is anywhere and everywhere.

There are, however, a few key websites you should be aware of while you are a member of the military family because *these sites* are the go-to DoD sources for the quality-of-life news that may affect you and your family. The content on a couple of them may seem rather "big military" to you right now, but that's okay.

BLUF? (Look it up in Appendix B if you don't know what means.)

Keep informed about things that matter to you, either now or in the future. That way, when you see practices and policies being put in place that make no sense at all to you, you can be that voice that says something about it.

It is in your unofficial job description, after all, to speak up as a military spouse and make sure others, to include policymakers, understand the facts.

Military OneSource, http://www.militaryonesource.com, is an important one, and you can read much more about it later in this chapter.

USA4MilitaryFamilies, www.usa4militaryfamilies.dod.mil, is the DoD site that shows you how effectively it is working with the states and nonprofits to effect real change on a macro level. Key issues are highlighted that affect members of the military family.

MILITARY FAMILY SUPPORT CENTERS

One of the most important resources you can know about when you are new to the military is the family support center. Military family support centers offer just what the name implies. Each branch of service has its own unique name for it, too.

Whether you are brand new in any community or you have been stabilized in one for a while, the family center offers you a range of programs and services.

Information and Referral (I&R)

You're new in town and don't know where to go to register your kids for childcare. You don't know where to find the nearest commissary. You need to figure out the duty bus schedule. You need a translator. You're trying to find a hotspot so you can check your mail or a landline to call someone. You want to talk to someone about writing a resume, or you need help with your finances.

The nice people who work at the I&R can either answer your questions or direct you to the service provider that can. They are well

Table 3.1.   Family Centers

In the:	It is known as:
Army	Army Community Service
Marine Corps	Marine Corps Community Services
Air Force	Airman and Family Readiness Center
Navy	Navy Fleet and Family Support
Coast Guard	Office of Work-Life Programs
National Guard/Reserves	Family Program

versed in community resources both on and off the military installation. They are usually the first faces you see when you step through the door of a family center, too.

Relocation Assistance Program (RAP)

Military life can involve multiple moves. When that time comes, you're sure to want to learn as much as you can about your soon-to-be new home before you get there and when you arrive.

The relocation assistance program at the nearest family support center can help you. They offer service members and families a long list of services.

Whether you are coming or going, your basic household items get packed and shipped out. The relocation assistance program has a *loan closet* where you can borrow basic household items such as microwave ovens, ironing boards, irons, dishes, and cookware while yours are en-route.

Many relocation assistance programs offer workshops, briefings, orientations, and sponsorship training so that new families can help plan and execute their moves and then feel welcome in their new location.

Foreign-born spouses may also learn about immigration and naturalization processes and participate in English-language classes.

In some service branches, the transition assistance program is included as a part of the relocation assistance program, too. The transition assistance program is designed to help military families make their final move when their time has come to do so.

Mobilization and Deployment Assistance (MOB/DEP)

Military mobilizations and deployments are an all-too-real part of military life. They are not easy on anyone, and that's where the family center's MOB/DEP program steps up and offers predeployment, mobilization, deployment, and redeployment briefings and support to service members, DoD civilians, and their families.

Also see chapter 6, "Dealing with Deployments and Other Separations."

Financial Readiness (FR)

Working with the experts in the Financial Readiness Program, service members and families can learn how to set and reach financial goals and address financial challenges. Topics commonly addressed include consumer education, budgeting and debt liquidation, retirement planning and savings, and investment counseling.

Financial readiness programs within the family support centers are often where individuals can turn for emergency financial assistance or to learn about federal financial assistance.

For more information about the services offered through the financial readiness program, see chapter 2, "Military Money and Benefits."

Employment Readiness Program (ERP)

Whether you are a spouse or transitioning service member seeking employment assistance, visit the employment readiness program where you can learn about local and global job opportunities as well as how to best apply for them. Many centers also offer a computer lab and career resource library for job seekers to use in their job search process.

Note to those in the Army family: service member mandatory transition assistance is provided through a separate program that doesn't fall under the family service umbrella, called the Soldier for Life Program (formerly known as the Army Career and Alumni Program or ACAP). Other service branches, however, generally incorporate their transition program within the family service center.

Family Advocacy Program (FAP)

Military life can be challenging and difficult on families and service members. The FAP understands this well and helps military service members and families to deal with those challenges.

The Family Advocacy Program helps military families to build and maintain healthy relationships through education and enrichment services. They offer workshops and services targeted to new and expectant parents. They offer emergency family assistance services and victim advocacy. They promote child safety and the prevention of child abuse and neglect. Some FAPs also offer respite care, safety education programs, self-defense classes, and so much more.

THE EXCEPTIONAL FAMILY MEMBER PROGRAM (EFMP)

The Exceptional Family Member Program (EFMP) helps those families with special needs children to identify and access services as they relocate within the military. Specifically, EFMP provides information and referral for military and community services. They educate the community about their many services through an active outreach program. They also work closely with local schools and early intervention services.

EFMP coordinators are instrumental in assisting families to make smooth transitions from place to place, and they also provide nonclinical case management such as creating individualized services plans.

You can find out more about EFMP by contacting the medical treatment facility on the installation you are currently stationed, or you can typically connect with them through the family support centers, too.

MILITARY CHILDCARE PROGRAMS

If you have children, you only want the best for them all the time. You especially want the best for them when you aren't the one watching over them while you work.

To that end, the DoD has a number of childcare programs available to military families both on and off the installation.

Child Development Centers (CDC) provides part- and full-time care for children from the age of six weeks old up until five years old. Located on the military installation, CDCs are usually open for business Monday through Friday, with some centers offering occasional evening care for a parents' night out.

In addition to facility care at CDCs, Family Child Care (FCC) homes are also an option usually available to you. FCC providers offer care for babies and children up to the age of twelve in their own homes. Providers must meet strict requirements and maintain current FCC certification to operate. Some FCC providers are able to offer extended care on evening and weekends.

Depending on where you are stationed, it may be difficult to secure a place for a child or children in the programs. Don't be surprised if there is a wait list involved.

If you are stuck on such a list or if you just want to consider it, off-installation childcare may be a more realistic option. The DoD has partnered with Childcare Aware of America (www.usa.childcareaware.org), which helps military families search for military-affiliated childcare off the installation.

School Age Care (SAC) programs are available for kids, too. From the ages of six to twelve, these programs provide care before and after school, on holidays, and during the school summer vacation time.

When your children morph into teenagers (twelve to eighteen years old), you still want to know that someone is keeping a good eye on them when you are unable to do so. On-installation teen and youth programs offer a variety of programs designed to both entertain and educate your teens.

Each branch of service issues fee guidance for its childcare services, but all are based on your total household income level.

You can locate information about available childcare options in your community of choice in a couple different ways.

You can visit http://www.militaryinstallations.dod.mil, or you can access MilitaryChildcare.com (MCC) at https://militarychildcare.cnic.navy.mil. MCC is a single online gateway that provides access to comprehensive information on military-operated and military-subsidized childcare options, full and part time, worldwide.

MORALE, WELFARE AND RECREATION (MWR)

Morale, Welfare and Recreation (MWR) programs and services strive to enhance the quality of life for service members, military retirees, civilian employees, their families, and other eligible participants. Without a doubt, the hard-working people behind the scenes and on the front lines of MWR do a fantastic job of it, too.

Examples of the types of programs and services included under the wide MWR umbrella include:

- fitness and sports centers
- libraries
- single service member programs and deployment support
- outdoor and indoor recreation centers
- leisure tours and travel
- auto hobby shops
- child and youth development programs (to include childcare services)
- skill development programs
- food and beverage establishments
- entertainment venues
- military clubs
- golf courses
- bowling centers
- marinas
- gaming machines

Some of MWR's programs and services are funded fully or partially thorough the DoD with an appropriated fund (APF), such as the family service centers and their many programs and the military library system. Others generate their revenues on the basis of their operations.

What does this mean for you?

You don't pay anything out of your own pocket to check out a library book or take advantage of classes, counseling, and other services through the family support center, while you do pay out of your own pocket to bowl, golf, rent a boat, or have a mocha latte at the resident coffee shop.

On the plus side, a percentage of the money earned by MWR through your self-pay patronage is funneled back into the community to provide you awesome things.

You have to be a military ID cardholder to use the MWR services.

To find out more about the MWR facilities available wherever you are stationed, visit your service branch's respective website.

- Army MWR (http://www.armymwr.com)
- Navy and Marine Corps MWR (http://www.navymwr.org)
- Coast Guard MWR (http://www.uscg.mil/mwr/)
- Air Force (http://www.usafservices.com/)

MILITARY ONESOURCE

Imagine a family support center solely online, and you must be imagining Military OneSource (http://www.militaryonesource.mil).

Military OneSource is a DoD-funded program that provides you information on every aspect of military life. It is a free online service for active duty, National Guard, and reserve members and their families. Think of Military OneSource as a virtual extension to installation family support services.

Call Center and Online Support

Over the phone or online, Military OneSource can give you suggestions and support for a huge range of issues, such as locating specific services in a community or improving your relationship with your spouse.

SPECIALTY CONSULTATIONS

You are able to take advantage of confidential specialty consultations with Military OneSource. They offer you access to trained and licensed counselors with expertise in areas such as wounded warrior issues, special needs, adult and elder care, finance, education, adoption, and health and wellness coaching.

Through the Military Family Life Counselors (MFLC), Military OneSource also offers confidential nonmedical counseling on a face-to-face, telephone, or online basis in such areas as stress management, relationships, grief, and parenting issues.

FINANCIAL SERVICES

You have access to short-term, solution-focused, and confidential financial counseling. Areas covered here include the following:

- money management and budgeting
- housing issues and loan concerns
- debt management, credit issues, and debt collection
- deployment and relocation-related financial issues
- Servicemembers Civil Relief Act (SCRA)
- investing basics and related tax issues
- mutual funds, IRAs, retirement planning, and insurance
- Thrift Savings Plan, 401(k), 403(b)
- DoD Savings Deposit Program

TAX SERVICES

With Military OneSource, you can file your federal taxes and state taxes for up to three states for free electronically.

They also provide, as a separate service, specialized confidential telephonic tax consultations with certified public accountants.

TRANSLATION SERVICES

Military OneSource provides language interpretation services and written translation of documents such as leases, marriage licenses, transcripts, and adoption paperwork.

SPOUSE EDUCATION AND
CAREER OPPORTUNITIES

Job-seeking spouses will find the access to expert education and career guidance that is provided online and telephonically by Military OneSource to be helpful.

The Spouse Education and Career Opportunities (SECO) program offers comprehensive information, tools, and resources to help you explore different career and education options and to help you make career connections.

ONLINE TOOLS, SOCIAL MEDIA, AND EDUCATIONAL MATERIALS

On the Military OneSource website, you will find ample on-demand content that touches upon each stage of military life.

Whether you are new to the military, single, married, and have children or not, or are coming to the end of your military career time, you can find useful information and strategies for navigating your way forward.

Military OneSource also has a Facebook page, a Twitter feed, and a Blog Brigade, which offers military spouses an opportunity to blog (and others to read and comment) about their "boots on the ground" experiences.

You can reach Military OneSource twenty-four hours a day, 365 days a year in a number of different ways.

Online: http://www.militaryonesource.com
Call from within the United States: 800-342-9647
Call from outside of the United States: 800-3429-6477 or 703-253-7599
Call collect from overseas: dial an international operator and ask to be connected to 703-253-7599
Call via voiceover Internet protocol: 800-842-9647
If you want to talk in Spanish: 877-888-0727
If you want to access via TTY/TDD: 866-607-6794
TTY/TDD in Spanish: 800-999-3004

THE COMMISSARY AND THE EXCHANGE

There are a number of shopping venues available to you within the military communities. Two of the biggies are the commissary and the installation exchange.

The commissary, if you don't know yet, is your grocery store, and it is run by the Defense Commissary Agency (DeCA). Commissaries are located worldwide on military installations and have been a great source of savings for military families for decades.

Like many of our services and programs of late, however, commissaries have been the targets of congressional cost-cutting efforts. Lucky for us, however, the proposed privatization of some stores seems to be off the table for the moment and the valued savings to military customers untouched. It's anyone's guess if commissaries will continue to exist as they do now in the future.

Take advantage of commissary shopping while you can.

At http://www.commissaries.com, you can read the latest sales flyer, and learn about the commissary rewards card that allows you to virtually clip coupons and enjoy savings. You can also find out when the latest and greatest case lot sale will be held in your community, and you find out if Click2Go Shop and Curbside Pickup is available in your area. You can also learn about any national food recalls and purchase gift cards on the site.

If you think of the commissary as a Costco equivalent, then you can think of The Exchange as a Target- or Walmart-like store. The Exchange offers preferred retail and services to military service members and their families the world over.

The Exchange funds 97 percent of its operating from the sale of goods and services. The remaining 3 percent comes through appropriated government funding. The nice thing about shopping at The Exchange is that two-thirds of what you spend there is paid back into the Army MWR and Air Force Service programs.

You can learn more about The Exchange at http://www.shopmy exchange.com.

Also interesting to note here: both the commissary and The Exchange are major employers of military families.

> Take advantage the perks available, such as resorts at the Hale Koa Hotel in Waikiki or the Edelweiss Lodge and Resort in Germany. Also take advantage of Space-A flights and discounted Disney and other theme park tickets.
>
> —Jessica Leia Moss, U.S. Coast Guard Brat and U.S. Air Force Spouse

DOD LODGING AND AFRC VACATION RESORTS

The DoD offers service members and families a number of temporary lodging possibilities. Each branch of service operates a hotel for your relocation and travel needs.

- Air Force Inns (http://af.dodlodging.net/)
- Army Lodging (http://www.armymwr.com/travel/lodging/de-fault.aspx)

- Inns of the Corps (http://www.innsofthecorps.com/index.html)
- Navy Gateway Inns and Suites (http://ngis.dodlodging.net/)
- Navy Getaways: RV Parks and Cottages (http://get.dodlodging. net/)
- Navy Lodge (https://www.navy-lodge.com/)

Affordable vacation getaways are also within reach, thanks to the Armed Forces Recreation Centers (AFRC), which provide access to four full-service resort hotels at enticing locations.

Learn more about each of the resorts below by accessing their website.

Shades of Green Walt Disney Resort
1950 West Magnolia Palm Drive, Lake Buena Vista, Florida 32830
Main Phone: (407) 824-3400
Reservations: (888) 593-2242
Attraction Hotline: (407) 824-1403
Web address: www.shadesofgreen.org

Edelweiss Lodge and Resort in Garmisch, Germany
St. Martin-Strasse 120, 82467 Garmisch-Partenkirchen
Unit 24501, APO AE 09006 (U.S. mailing address for resort)
Main Phone: +49 8221-9440
Reservations: call main phone or reserve online. Note: review eligibility rules carefully. A 2015 review of German host nation laws narrowed the scope of who may legally stay here.
Vacation Planning: +49 8221-9440
Web address: http://www.edelweisslodgeandresort.com

Hale Koa Hotel, Honolulu, Hawaii
2055 Kalia Road, Honolulu, Hawaii 96815
Reservation Information: book online at http://www.halekoa.com
Commercial Telephone: 800-367-6027
DSN Telephone: 315-438-6739

Dragon Hill Lodge, Seoul, Korea
Unit 15335, APO AP 96205
Reservations: reservations@dhl.korea.army.mil
Commercial Telephone: (011-82-2)7918-222
DSN Telephone: 738-2222
Web address: http://www.dragonhilllodge.com

ARMED FORCES ENTERTAINMENT

In times of peace or war, the Armed Forces Entertainment and the United Services Organization (USO), http://www.uso.org, raise morale by bringing first-class entertainment to troops and their families stationed overseas whether they are located in remote locations, on ships at seas, or elsewhere performing contingency operations.

If you find yourself stationed overseas at some point, you're sure to appreciate the fine and varied entertainment provided by AFE and the USO.

For a list of the current tour schedule, visit http://www.armedforces entertainment.com/schedule/.

MILITARY FAMILY SUPPORT OUTSIDE THE DOD

There are reportedly over twenty-seven thousand organizations outside the military that offer support on multiple levels to military families. While the following list is far from comprehensive, it does highlight some organizations that you are likely to hear about in your journey in and around the military:

- Air Force Aid Society (http://www.afas.org)
- American Freedom Foundation (http://www.americanfreedom foundation.org)
- American Legion (http://www.legion.org)
- American Military Partner Association (http://www.military partners.org)
- American Red Cross (http://www.redcross.org)
- Army Emergency Relief (http://www.aerhq.org)
- Blue Star Families (http://www.bluestarfam.org)
- Bob Woodruff Family Foundation (http://www.bobwoodruff foundation.org)
- Coast Guard Mutual Assistance (http://www.cqmahq.org)
- Corporate America Supports You (http://www.casy.msccn.org)
- Disabled American Veterans (http://www.dav.org)
- Fisher House Foundation (http://www.fisherhouse.org)
- Habitat for Humanity (http://www.habitat.org)
- Hearts Apart (http://www.heartsapart.org)
- Home Front Hearts (http://www.homefronthearts.org)
- Homes for Our Troops (http://www.hfotusa.org)

- Hope for the Warriors (http://www.hopeforthewarrior.org)
- In Gear Career (http://www.ingearcareer.org)
- Intrepid Fallen Heroes Fund (http://www.fallenheroesfund.org)
- Iraq & Afghanistan Veterans of America (http://www.iava.org)
- Military Child Education Coalition (http://www.mcec.org)
- Military Family Advisory Network (http://www.militaryfamily advisorynetwork.org)
- Military Officers Association of America (http://www.moaa.org)
- Military Spouses of Strength (http://www.milspousesofstrength.org)
- National Military Family Association (http://www.militaryfamily. org)
- Naval Services FamilyLine (http://www.nsfamilyline.org)
- Navy Marine Corps Relief Society (http://www.nmcrs.org)
- Operation Care and Comfort (http://www.occ-usa.org)
- Operation Homefront (http://www.operationhomefront.net/)
- Operation Support Our Troops America (http://www.osotamerica .org)
- Our Military Kids (http://ourmilitarykids.org)
- Pat Tillman Foundation (http://www.pattillmanfoundation.org)
- SaveandInvest (http://www.saveandinvest.org)
- Semper Fi Fund (https://semperfifund.org)
- Silver Star Families of America (http://www.silverstarfamilies.org)
- Soldiers Angels (http://www.soldiersangels.org)
- Thanks USA (http://www.thanksusa.org)
- The Generals Kids (http://www.thegeneralskids.org)
- The Seal-NSW Family Foundation (www.sealnswff.org)
- They Serve 2 (http://www.theyserve2.org)
- Toys for Tots Foundation (http://www.toysfortots.org)
- Tragedy Assistance Program for Survivors (http://www.taps.org)
- United Services Organization (USO) (http://www.uso.org)
- United Through Reading (http://www.unitedthroughreading.org)
- USACares (www.usacares.org)
- USO (http://www.uso.org)
- Veterans of Foreign Wars (http://www.vfw.org)
- Veterans Moving Forward (http://www.vetsfwd.org)
- Wounded Warriors Family Support (http://www.wwfs.org)
- Wounded Warrior Project (http://www.woundedwarriorproject .org)

More Spousal and Family Non-DoD Sources of Support

- Army Wives Network (http://www.armywifenetwork.com)
- Home Front United Network (http://www.homefrontunited.com)
- Macho Spouse (http://malemilspouse.com)
- Making It in the MilLife (http://www.moaablogs.org/spouse/)
- Military Spouse JD Network (http://www.msjdn.org)
- *Military Spouse* Magazine (http://www.militaryspouse.com)
- Military Transition News (http://online.militarytransitionnews.com)
- National Military Spouse Network (http://www.nationalmilitary spousenetwork.com)
- NextGen MilSpouse (http://www.nextgenmilspouse.com)
- Operation We Are Here (http://www.operationwearehere.com)
- SpouseBUZZ (http://www.spousebuzz.com)
- USMC Life (http://www.usmclife.com)

4

MASTERING MILITARY MOVES

Crappy assignment? It's temporary.
Dream assignment? It's temporary.

—Kristin M. Sells, U.S. Air Force Brat and U.S. Army Spouse

In your military travels, should you move someplace you don't particularly enjoy or meet someone you don't particularly like, don't worry. Sooner or later, somebody will get orders to move.

Of course, the irony is that you might see them again at the next place. Walt Disney, it turns out, was right. *It is a small world, after all.*

Moving is a huge and interesting part of military life. In this world, *permanent change of station* (PCS) orders move service members and families on the average of every two to three years. Those orders can take you to the other side of the state, the country, or clear across the world.

Try to obtain a sponsor through the gaining unit who can help facilitate a smooth transition.

—Jennifer Oswalt, U.S. Air Force Spouse

The caveat, if you will, is that you don't always get to choose where you want to move. You move where the military needs your service member the most. That place can be as exciting as Europe or as unexciting as [insert your worst-feared location here].

Not to get your hopes up too much, but service members do sometimes get to request their assignments and select their next duty station. That doesn't always happen, though. There are several factors that could be taken into consideration, to include the service member's skill set, time in service, and the needs of Uncle Sam that can best be served.

> Learn what you can about your new home before arriving.
>
> —Jennifer Oswalt, U.S. Air Force Spouse

If you have or are anticipating PCS orders to a specific location and you want to know more about your soon-to-be new home, turn first to DoD Military Installations, online at http://www.militaryinstallations.dod .mil/MOS/f?p=MI:ENTRY:0. This is the DoD's official source for installation and state resources available to active duty, guard, and reserve service and family members.

> Look at your whole family when it comes to requesting and accepting assignments. How independent are your family members? What are the requirements of the new duty station/assignment, and how will that impact the service member's ability to be with and provide support to the family? What else is going on in the extended family? Is someone going to need your assistance in the near term (major illnesses, pending death)? There are many "dream" assignments and locations. They usually stop being a dream if the family requirements exceed the resources a service member can apply.
>
> —Kate Numerick, USA Soldier and USA Spouse

THERE IS A DOWNSIDE TO MOVING

While it's exciting to experience new places and meet new people, moving can also take a real toll on everyone in the family, especially school-aged children who certainly didn't sign up for this lifestyle voluntarily and who end up changing schools and friends more often than any kid should have to in the course of a lifetime.

Professionally minded military spouses also face a fair share of job search stress, too, as families who are accustomed to having two paychecks to draw upon are once again reduced to only one until the boxes are unpacked and a new job is found.

Not only is moving hard on the family, it's not exactly easy on the wallet, either. Of course, there are moving allowances designed to offset the costs; however, it never seems like quite enough when you're shelling out the bucks left and right.

The stress often associated with moving can be minimized through careful planning, however. It doesn't hurt to have a healthy sense of adventure and superhuman powers of flexibility, either.

While you may not be able to imagine it right now, many who eventually separate from service or retire admit to missing the process of packing up and moving on to new adventures the most. It's called the "three-year itch."

Don't be surprised if you end up getting it, too.

> We have been stationed all over the United States and Germany. Make time to travel and get to know the area you live in.
>
> —Rebecca Roth, U.S. Air Force Spouse

COORDINATING YOUR MILITARY MOVE

You might only think there are four seasons that include spring, summer, fall, and winter, but there is also a fifth season in the military. It is called PCS season, and it generally happens during the summer months, when the kids are out of school for the summer.

While the summer months are typically busy moving months for military families, PCS moves can happen any time of the year.

There are times when you don't know for sure when they are going to happen. You may have a good idea and even have what you believe to be an accurate date marked on the calendar. Don't be surprised, however, if the military has different plans for your service member.

> Expect the unexpected. Just when they tell you not to expect orders, you'll get them to Germany.
>
> —Jessica Leia Moss, U.S. Coast Guard Brat and U.S. Air Force Spouse

Sooner or later, however, you will have orders, and you will need to start making your PCS move a reality. Your first step will be to coordinate your move with the local military transportation office, or TO, for short.

Table 4.1.   Transportation Office Names by Service Branch

Army	Installation Transportation Office
Navy	Personal Property Shipping Office
Marine Corps	Personal Property Shipping Office
Air Force	Traffic Management Office
Coast Guard	Household Goods Shipping Office
DoD/Joint Forces	Joint Personal Property Shipping Office

You'll want to meet with them and discuss exactly how your stuff will get moved from where it is now to where it needs to be.

Don't procrastinate about contacting the transportation office. Remember that other people are PCSing, too, particularly in the May to August time frames. It is known as the PCS season. If you are planning to move around that busy PCS season, too, then you'll want to beat the crowd or at least get your spot in the lineup of moves as soon as possible.

Once you have confirmed appointments for your moving days, try not to change them unless you want to risk throwing off your entire timeline of moving events.

That initial contact to the TO can be done in person on the military installation, or your sponsor can create an account online at http://www .move.mil and conduct what is called self-counseling. Please note, however, online self-counseling at http://www.move.mil may not be an option available to you if this is your first or last PCS move or if other extenuating circumstances exist.

You can be the one to coordinate the move, too, assuming you have a PSC-specific Power of Attorney or Letter of Authority in hand. You can get these legal documents free of charge at the installation legal office.

Before you and/or your sponsor go to the TO, have a good idea of when you want to move and how much estimated weight you will have. See "Weighty Matters" later in this chapter for more information.

Try to be as flexible as possible concerning your potential packout dates. Don't make the mistake of combining your packout dates with dates for other big tasks such as turning over your rental property. You just don't need that kind of stress. *You feel?*

Know what's going on in your life before you show up at the TO. It will make your experience there far more meaningful to you.

For example, know *when* you plan to arrive at your new duty station and what items you need to ship or have stored in the process. Let them know if you have any uniquely sized items that require special packing.

Write down any questions you have that you don't know the answer to and ask them those questions when you visit them.

This is also a good time to visit the Plan My Move application on Military OneSource at https://apps.militaryonesource.mil/MOS/f?p= PMM:ENTRY:0.

Plan My Move allows you to create a custom moving plan and calendar. It also gives you access to information about your potential benefits and entitlements in the moving process.

We'll also go over some of that in "Potential Moving Benefits and Entitlements," later in this chapter.

In the military moving process, there will also be informative PCS move and finance briefings that your sponsor must attend.

You may also be welcome to attend, and if you are, *go* without fail. Take copious notes and ask lots of questions. Two heads are always better than one when it comes to handling a family move.

Before you leave your current duty station for the next, your sponsor will probably be required to *out process* the installation. In other words, he will carry around a checklist to all of the major offices on the installation and get them to *clear* (initial and/or place a stamp of approval) his departure from the installation.

After you've PCSed a few times, you can always tell who is clearing on an installation by the telltale black briefcases and the look of desperation on their faces.

> Once you arrive, get involved! While you don't want to overcommit— especially right at first—it is also important not to allow yourself to become isolated. Even if you are not typically a social person, search out ways to meet others. Utilize social media, churches, the active duty member's new unit, and your new installation newspaper, website, or radio station to find local groups. Get to know your neighbors—they can become great friends and people you can count on.
>
> —Jennifer Oswalt, U.S. Air Force Spouse

Big Decisions, Smart Actions

As you plan and plot your move, you'll need to decide whether you are going to have the government move you or you are going to move yourself. You will also need to decide whether you are going to ship a car or not. And of course, you'll want to start thinking about where you will actually live when you get there.

Do you want to live in military housing on the installation itself, or would you prefer to live off the installation within the local community and collect BAH? (See chapter 2, "Military Money and Benefits," for more information about the Basic Allowance for Housing.)

Understand that the rules and regulations where you are PCSing to may, in fact, make the housing decisions for you. For instance, you may be required to live in government housing if it is available or if you are of a certain rank.

Table 4.2.   Frequently Used Military Moving Terms

PCS Move	Permanent Change of Station
TO	Transportation Office
PPTM	Personally Procured Transportation Moves (formerly Do It Yourself or DITY)
POV	Personally Owned Vehicle
UAB	Unaccompanied Baggage
BAH	Basic Housing Allowance
OHA	Overseas Housing Allowance
DLA	Dislocation Allowance
MALT	Monetary Allowance in Lieu of Transportation
MIHA	Move-In Housing Allowance
TLA	Temporary Lodging Allowance
TLE	Temporary Lodging Expense

Defense Personal Property Program (DP3):
Your one-stop, 24/7 source for managing personal property moves online. (Access them by first obtaining a login and password at www.move.mil.)

Full Replacement Value (FRV):
What you hope you get reimbursed if your valuables are lost or damaged beyond repair.

Household Goods (HHG):
The stuff you own that must go from one duty station to the next.

Joint Travel Regulations (JTF):
The military rules that govern your official travel and transportation.

Transportation Office (TO):
Your main point of contact on either side of the moving van.

Transportation Service Provider (TSP):
The commercial moving company you trust with your stuff.

Unaccompanied Baggage (UB):
The lightweight, must-have essentials you need to set up your household. They are shipped ahead of your HHG.

My advice would be to always make the best of each and every duty station no matter how big, how close, or how far. We've had the good fortune of living in some really wonderful and unique places, but our very first duty station was on the Gulf Coast of Mississippi. Definitely not our first choice, but it ended up being a fun two years in an area of the country I may have never made it to. The friends we made there as a young Navy family are still our friends now.

—Heather Smith, U.S. Navy Spouse

POTENTIAL MOVING
BENEFITS AND ENTITLEMENTS

The DoD will foot the bill to move you and your family. In order to receive any payments, your sponsor will need to go through the necessary finance channels to make it happen.

In the PCS process, you may be eligible for a travel per diem for each member of your family. As of 2016, service members get $140 per day of travel while eligible family members over the age of twelve get 75 percent of the service member's applicable rate and 50 percent for each family member under the age of twelve.

Service members are also entitled to a Dislocation Allowance (DLA) to cover some of the expenses incurred in relocating a household on a PCS move. DLA may be paid in advance, and it is in addition to any other allowances authorized in the Joint Federal Travel Regulation (JTFR).

The amount of DLA one receives is based on the service member's rank and whether he has dependents (that would be *family members*) or not.

For example, in 2016 an E-1 without family members would receive $912.20 as his DLA. With dependents, he would receive $2,113.50. An O-1, on the other hand, would receive $1,628.38 without dependents and $2,209.47 with dependents.

You can access the current DLA rates by visiting http://www.defensetravel.dod.mil/site/otherratesDLA.cfm.

When it comes to the amounts being paid out, just know that there are regulations galore, subject to change, which dictate who gets how much for whatever point is in question.

Just to complicate matters, each branch of the service has their own list of charts that they follow when doling out payments, and they don't always match each other, either.

Even with the DoD's generous moving allowances, you're going to need to be prepared financially for out-of-pocket expenses sure to pop up along the way. The sooner you can create a moving budget that includes an estimate of your moving expenses and add savings to it, the better.

Things Might Change

In keeping with congressional cost-cutting *force of the future* efforts, don't be surprised if one day soon the current way PCS moves occur change significantly.

As you might guess, it costs big bucks to move service members and their families all over the place every two to three years.

According to one source, the average cost of a military PCS move runs about $6,700.00, up 28 percent from 2001's average of $4,200.[1]

As more cost-cutting measures are aggressively sought out and eventually implemented, service members could wind up experiencing fewer PCS moves in their careers as a result, saving Uncle Sam big dollars in the process.

Ironically, the DoD might get bonus points with that approach as military spouses who work in jobs they like wouldn't have to leave them as frequently and families accustomed to having two paychecks could continue to have two paychecks longer, promoting enhanced financial readiness.

> Don't look at your home as temporary, although it probably is. If you spend the whole time at one station waiting on what is next to come, then you won't appreciate your current situation! There are many adventures in the military. You can choose to focus on the negatives or enjoy the positives.
>
> —Hannah Schlagel, U.S. Army Spouse

WEIGHTY MATTERS

Without trying too hard, you can collect a lot of things over time. Some of those things you can get rid of before your PCS move because you no longer like them, want them, or use them. They don't hold sentimental value, and they will only add to the weight of your *household goods* (HHG) shipment.

Excess weight can cost *you* (not the military, but you personally) big, big bucks.

The DoD pays for your move, but it will only pay up to a certain weight limit. If you go over that limit, you get to pay for the rest of it, and it can be expensive to the tune of several hundred to several thousand dollars.

According to current, and, of course, subject-to-change regulations, the minimum excess cost is about $100 per one hundred pounds over the allowance.

Exactly how much can you ship on the government's dime?

The answer depends on your service member's rank and how many family members are involved. Look at table 4.3 Basic HHG Weight Allowances for details.

Try to correctly estimate your HHG weight and do your best to stay within the coverable allowances.

How do you do it without having an industrial-sized scale?

It's easy. You can guesstimate one thousand pounds per room, not including any storage rooms or bathrooms. To that estimated guess, add the estimated weight of large appliances and other heavy items you own.

About Your Professional Gear

There are some weight-saving techniques you can use, too.

Service members can subtract up to two thousand pounds net weight of professional books, papers, and equipment (PBP&E/PRO-GEAR).

Table 4.3.   Basic HHG Weight Allowances (Extracted from Defense Transportation Regulation, Part IV, Personal Property, February 23, 2010.)

Grade	With Dependents	Without Dependents
O-10 to O-6	18,000	18,000
O-5/W-5	17,500	16,000
O-4/W-4	17,000	14,000
O-3/W-3	14,500	13,000
O-2/W-2	13,500	12,500
O-1/W-1/Service Academy Graduates	12,000	10,000
E-9	15,000*	13,000*
E-8	14,000	12,000
E-7	13,000	11,000
E-6	11,000	8,000
E-5	9,000	7,000
E-4	8,000	7,000
E-3 to E-1	8,000	5,000
Aviation Cadets	8,000	7,000
Service Academy Cadets & Midshipmen		350

*Very senior enlisted positions may have different allowances.

These are items defined as HHG items in a service member's possession that are needed for the performance of official duties at the next or a later destination.

If you have PBP&E/PRO-GEAR, then be sure you tell the moving counselor at the TO about it so they can be noted on the correct form called a DD 1299 and later deducted from the weight of your shipment.

Be forewarned now. There is a lot of paperwork involved in a PCS move, too.

In addition to letting the moving counselor at transportation know about your professional gear, you also need to physically separate those items from your HHG shipment before or on moving day so the movers can pack, mark, and weigh the items separately.

Before you gleefully think you can count the hundreds of pounds of workout weights in your basement as professional gear, think again. Examples of PBP&E/PRO-GEAR items include work-related reference material, professional instruments, specialized clothing, and some communications equipment. It does *not* include sports equipment, office and/or household furniture, commercial products, shop fixtures, personal computers and associated equipment, memorabilia, and table servings.

What about the stuff you need for *your* job? Military spouses may also be authorized up to five hundred pounds of PBP&E/PRO-GEAR as well.

Know What You Can Ship and What You Can't

There are strict rules about what you can ship in your HHG and what you can't. See tables 4.4 and 4.5 for a list of items, respectively.

Table 4.4.   Things You Can't Ship in Your HHGs

Personal baggage when carried free on commercial transportation
Automobiles, trucks, vans, and other motor vehicles
Airplanes, mobile homes, camper trailers, horse trailers, and farming vehicles
Live animals including birds, fish, and reptiles
Things that would normally quality as HHG but you get them after you're PCS
Replacement HHG items
Cordwood and building materials
HHGs that you want to use for resale, dispose of, or use in a commercial business
Privately owned ammunition
Hazardous materials such as explosives, flammables, corrosives, poisons, and
  propane gas tanks
Gypsy moths

Table 4.5. Things You Can Ship in Your HHG

Personal property
Personal effects
Professional items
Spare car parts
Consumable goods
Vehicles other than cars
Boat or watercraft
Ultralight vehicle
Utility trailer
Professional clothing
Alcoholic beverages

Get your HHG shipment weighed before it leaves and when it arrives. You can also request a reweigh on either end of your move at no cost. Why? You want to be sure the weight stays the same. You don't want to end up inadvertently paying for someone else's stuff.

Unaccompanied or Whole Baggage

In addition to your HHG, you might also be eligible for a shipment of *unaccompanied baggage* (UB) or *whole baggage*, as it is also called.

UB is a shipment of essential items you might need right away such as kitchenware, weather-appropriate clothes, and other lightweight household items. There is usually a weight limit for your whole baggage, too.

> Accompany the active duty member to newcomers' briefings and culture orientations. Many installations offer a certain amount of free childcare for inbound families if needed.
>
> —Jennifer Oswalt, U.S. Air Force Spouse

Other Shipping Points to Note

Full costs may or may not be paid by the government for the shipment or storage of boats, motorcycles, booze, and weapons.

If you are moving to a remote location where, for example, your favorite cereal cannot be obtained, you may even be authorized to ship up to 1,250 pounds of suitable consumable goods per tour year.

Prepare Your HHG for Shipment

- Have any expensive and valuable items you own appraised. Uncle Sam won't pay for those appraisals, but you'll appreciate having proof of purchase price if your valuables go missing or are damaged or repairs are required. Keep the original purchase receipts for your more expensive items separate from your shipments, too.
- Create a video home inventory of your possessions. Record closeup shots of your furniture, the working condition of your electronics, and the actual appearance of your high-dollar valued items prior to moving day.
- Identify and plan to hand carry small and/or extremely valuable items such as stocks, bonds, jewelry, coins, and coin collections. Don't trust anyone else with irreplaceable items such as photo albums. Pack those in your suitcase along with purchase receipts, pictures, and appraisals.
- Donate or sell the excess you no longer want, need, or use.
- If you've moved before, be sure to remove old moving stickers left on items from your last PCS move so things don't get confusing this time around. Consider saving some from each move to create a keepsake project such as holiday ornament covered in moving stickers or a framed collage.
- Pull items to be moved out of the attic, crawlspace, or from any other hard-to-reach and potentially unsafe-to-reach areas. The movers won't go there for you.
- Ensure your UB, HHG, and PBP&E/PRO-GEAR items are separated.
- Empty and defrost your refrigerator and/or freezer at least two days before movers arrive. Make sure items are completely dry and cleaned. Get rid of any foods that could spoil or spill in transit or when stored.
- If you have a hot tub or waterbed, drain the water from them.
- If you have a window air conditioner that will be shipped, remove it from the window before they get there.
- Take anything that is fixed on the wall off the wall.
- Tape hardware to the back of items that need it with duct tape. You'll be ever so glad you did on the other end of the move.
- Drain the gas, oil, and/or water out of any power equipment you are shipping.

- Understand what is reimbursable and what isn't.
- Clean your car and prepare it for shipping if moving overseas.
- Arrange for storage of HHG, vehicles, or any other items you don't plan to move with you.
- Make sure your goods are insured as they move from one place to another. You may have renters' insurance already that covers this. Confirm that and/or talk to the TO counselor about coverage if you don't have it.
- Separate important papers and items that you plan to hand carry. Such papers include moving documents, birth certificates, and medical records, shot records, passports, or any work-related credentials you may need to find a job.

PCS moves can be complicated, but they are not impossible. After you've arranged for one, you'll have a better idea what to expect the next time. Just be sure you work closely with the transportation office counselors and you and your stuff should be fine.

> If you can't pack it, don't buy it or wait [to get it later]. Things get broken during moves. You WILL move.
>
> —Jessica Leia Moss, U.S. Coast Guard Brat and U.S. Air Force Spouse

BEYOND BOXES: PREPARING FOR YOUR MOVE

Moving involves far more than boxing up your household goods, of course.

Moving is a process where you simultaneously close out one chapter of your life while beginning another. In between where one home ends and the other begins, in what can be described as a nomadic and unnerving Twilight Zone, is one very long and eclectic list of things you have to do.

As previously noted, Military OneSource (http://www.militaryone source.mil) can help you manage your move with its Plan My Move application. It offers you printable checklists and gives you the tools to compare the cost of living between communities, locate jobs and schools, and explore neighborhoods.

That said, you can never have too many lists.

Before You Leave Your Current Location

- Coordinate your exit, travel, and arrival plans.
- Establish and save dollars in a moving fund.
- Keep track of tax-deductible moving expenses.
- Begin to use up household supplies unless you are planning to ship them.
- If you are renting now, review your lease and make sure you give the landlord adequate notice. If you are a homeowner and want to sell, contact a Realtor or consider renting your property out. Interview prospective property managers well in advance.
- Arrange for utilities to be turned off, and cancel local subscriptions.
- Notify those who need to know of your new address, including the transportation office that might not have this information yet because you didn't have it yet. You want to see your valued possessions once again, right?
- Determine what you need to do to bring your pets along with you.
- Keep your bills paid on time throughout the moving process.
- Monitor your bank accounts. You don't need any nasty surprises now.
- Start your online job search now if work is in your future plans.
- Start your online search for new living arrangements now.
- Research school districts for your kids and make inquiries now.
- If you have preteens or teenagers, try to connect them with their new school and/or new contacts in that area that may be able to help make their transition easier.
- Plan to see or do things in your current area that you have been meaning to all along. Your time there is running out, and you don't want regrets later.

> PCSing is a very stressful time, even more so when you're employed. Having a financial nest egg to fall back on will alleviate some of that stress.
>
> —Pam Cabana Macken, U.S. Air Force Spouse (Retired) and
> U.S. Air Force Brat

MOVING DAY TO-DO LISTS

You coordinated your PCS move with transportation in a timely manner, and you have begun the bittersweet process of closing out life in one place and starting it in another. If you have one more yard sale, Ebay may attempt a hostile takeover.

Kudos to you, master organizer of your universe. Things are falling into place.

You are clearly making significant progress, but don't rest on your PCS laurels just yet. There is still much work to be accomplished. The launching of the doves en masse and the popping of the cork on the chilled champagne will have to wait.

The movers are coming.

Twice.

Stay with your movers as they pack/unpack your things. Oversight is a great deterrent to unfortunate circumstances. Some people supply snacks and drinks, which is a nice gesture.

—Jennifer Oswalt, U.S. Air Force Spouse

The Day the Movers Take It All Away

- Before the movers come, disconnect the electronics such as your satellite dish, stereo, and other big appliances.
- Dismantle any outdoor equipment that is being shipped. Make sure it is bug-free, specifically, *gypsy moth*–free. Gypsy moths are apparently big-time, freeloading, leaf-eating caterpillars that destroy trees and plant life.
- Ensure that your valuables are secured (i.e., jewelry and important paperwork).
- Designate a mover-free safe zone in a closet or bathroom and put a *do not enter* sign up. Keep anything there that you don't want the movers to take. Lock it if possible.
- If you have small children or potentially stressed-out pets, arrange for them to be somewhere else out of the line of fire that day. Everyone will be grateful for it in the long run.
- Supervise the movers to ensure items are being wrapped properly. If you don't think they're doing a good job, call the transportation office and tell them so. They should send someone out to see what's going on.
- Ensure all items are labeled specifically and accurately on the inventory sheets. This is truly a pain to do, not because it is a difficult

thing to do. It's a pain because by the time you get to this point of the day, you just want the movers to leave your presence never to return. You don't even mind, for a crazy fleeting moment, if you ever see your stuff again. Take a deep breath and then make sure everything is noted correctly.

- Be sure you agree with the mover's description of the state of your items. There is a guide to the symbols used on the inventory form. Read it. If you don't agree, state that in writing in the exceptions section of the form. Don't get feisty with the lead mover doing the paperwork, either. He doesn't get paid enough, and he is about to drive off with every one of your valued possessions. Just call the TO if there appears to be unresolvable issues.
- Make sure all items are packed on-site unless you have discussed other arrangements with the TO.
- Watch as items are loaded on the truck. Be sure heavy items aren't loaded on top of lighter ones.
- Make certain serial numbers are correctly noted on the inventory sheets.
- While you aren't required to provide lunch or refreshments for the hard-working movers, it's a common practice to do so. Not only is it a nice thing to do, but it may also go a long way to making sure your stuff is well cared for in the process. Bonus points if you ask them what they want instead of assuming pizza and burgers, which they probably get enough of each week.

Most importantly, be sure that your household goods are arranged in an organized and logical way—kitchen items in the kitchen, bathroom items in the bathroom, for example—to help ensure that like items are packed together, which makes unpacking much easier. As movers unpack your items, you will know right where they go.

—Jennifer Oswalt, U.S. Air Force Spouse

The Day the Movers Bring Everything Back

- Know in advance where you want the boxes and furniture to go in your new home away from home.
- Check each item off the inventory as it is unloaded from the truck. Make sure everything on the inventory is accounted for before the movers leave.

- Note any damage or loss at the time of delivery, using the assigned inventory number, on DD Form 1840, Joint Statement of Loss or Damage. The movers will have copies of this form.
- If you have missing or damaged items, there is a claims process you can initiate within nine months of delivery. The new TO can help you do that.

Establish communication with loved ones back home as soon as possible. Knowing that your support network is only a phone call or message away can be very comforting. Find those free wi-fi spots and connect! Go explore!

—Jennifer Oswalt, U.S. Air Force Spouse

When You Arrive at Your New Location

- Arrange for telephone service, Internet connectivity, water, cable/DIRECTV, and garbage pickup service. Keep track of deposits made so you can get them back later.
- Inspect any property you plan to rent or purchase carefully. Be sure you're satisfied that everything is in acceptable working order. Make notes on lease or purchase documents identifying any damage now before you take control of it.
- Close out the business of moving. Once your HHG and UB items are delivered, inspect them closely. File a claim for those things that didn't make it or were damaged. Contact the TO in your new location to find out how to do that.
- Update your existing insurance policies to cover your new home and all the things inside it.
- Visit the local Department of Motor Vehicles (DMV) to get a new driver's license. Bring a healthy dose of patience and something to read while you wait because you know you're going to wait.
- Get new license plates and/or tags for your car.
- Register to vote unless you are voting absentee from another state.
- Make sure your change-of-address instructions are working and update as necessary.
- Sign up for local newspaper delivery, virtually or otherwise.
- Figure out who the go-to service providers will be in your new community. For example, identify the nearest hospital, family doctor, dentist, banker, vet, and hairstylist . . . not necessarily in that order.

- If you have children, get them settled as soon as possible. Register them in school and enroll them in extracurricular activities so they can start the important business of forming friendships.
- Explore your new hometown and its culture with an open mind. Who knows? You might end up actually liking sweet tea, lobster rolls, or fish tacos.

> Choose your friends wisely and carefully; the military is a small community.
>
> —Aubrey Kaufman, DoD Civilian Employee

MOVING WITH SMALL CHILDREN AND TEENAGERS

Moving is hard enough on you and your spouse. Imagine how hard it will be on your kids of any age, if you happen to have them. Even if by some miracle they are excited about moving, it can still be difficult as they say goodbye to good friends and a routine life and start over somewhere unfamiliar without either.

During a PCS move, it's important to keep age-appropriate lines of communication open with your children at all times. No doubt they will have many questions. You may not always have the answers to give them, and that can be tough.

While you don't want to upset your kids with all the indecision and uncertainty that can accompany at PCS move, you don't want to keep them in the dark, either.

Encourage your children to keep an open mind. Remind them that they will still be able to connect with their friends on social media.

Figure out whether they will have friends there that they already know. The nice thing about being a military brat is that you often run into the same friends at different times.

Actively involve your children in the transition process. Talk about where it is you're moving to and make a list of the places you want to visit nearby and the things you want to try in the new community. Give them something to look forward to when you arrive.

Let them be upset if they are upset. They may need to have a good cry, and there's nothing wrong with that, either.

Realize, early on, that your kids are going to follow your lead. How you frame the experience will be how they live it. If you are unhappy about your pending PCS, they will be unhappy, too. If you are excited and seem to look forward to it, chances are that they will be more receptive to the move as well.

> Every time you move, after you have unpacked all your boxes, take the time to find a place to volunteer in your new community. The benefits are enormous to you, your family and your community, as you will feel a self of belonging right away. There is no better way to make your new community your home.
>
> —Carmen Carlisle, U.S. Marine Corps Spouse

BRINGING FURRY FAMILY MEMBERS ALONG

Family pets may not show up on your official PCS orders but, if you're like many, you consider them an important part of your family. Moving can be stressful on them, too. Just like children, they seem to have a real sense of impending change, and they usually don't like it, either.

If you are being transferred in the continental United States, you may be able to drive Fido or Garfield wherever you're going. Or not. You may have to figure out how to ship your furry baby to your new duty station.

If you have an exotic pet, there may even be other transportation requirements and specific regulations to be aware of before the big day arrives.

If you are being transferred overseas, you need to make sure you can take your pet in the first place. Some countries have travel and breed restrictions or require extended periods of quarantine where you are responsible for paying for boarding.

If you do take your pet overseas, remember you have to bring him back, too. The military may not be able to accommodate the shipping of your pet from OCONUS back the United States. You may be required to pay big bucks to have Fido shipped home privately.

Wherever you're going, these tips may help to make the move for your pet easier:

- Microchip your pet and make sure your pet wears a collar and ID tags that have your contact information.
- If your animal is taking mediations, be sure you have a good supply on hand.

- If flights will be involved, be sure you contact the airline well ahead of time to find out what kind of pet carrier will be required. Be sure it is well ventilated and your pet has access to water. Research their pet shipping success rate. Realize that some airlines will not allow certain breeds of dogs to fly at any time. Others may have restrictions on when pets can seasonally fly.
- Be sure your pet is up to date on all shots. Depending on where you are traveling, you may need to have dated health certificates. Always check in advance. You don't want to assume something only to find out you can't bring your pet at the last minute.
- Keep your pet on a leash at all times.
- Have a backup pet travel care plan. You can make what you believe to be all the necessary arrangements only to be told it's a no go for Fido on flight day. What would you do in that case? Think about your options now and plan accordingly.
- Never abandon the family pet. You'd think that would go without saying, but it does happen in military communities, particularly when families are stationed overseas and need to return to the United States. Instead, investigate rehoming options or temporary boarding arrangements.

If you have pets, or are considering getting a puppy or a kitten, follow the import guidelines of the strictest country with regards to microchipping, rabies shots, etc. Keep all the documentation organized in a file. You never know what your next duty assignment will be. If you do this from the start, your pet will be ready to go when you are.

—Pam Cabana Macken, U.S. Air Force (Retired) and
U.S. Air Force Brat

IF YOU'RE MOVING OVERSEAS

If you are truly lucky, at some point you will have the opportunity to PCS overseas. Living in a different country gives you and your family a wonderful chance to experience a new culture, try new foods, travel, and meet people who may or may not think like you or be like you.

It is a fantastic, life-enriching experience if you're open to it.

Not all overseas assignments are created equally, however. While it may come down to personal preferences in the end, no one can argue that

When you first arrive in your new location, consider making small excursions to local restaurants or shopping centers. Once you have built up confidence and become more familiar with your surroundings, embark upon grander adventures.

—Jennifer Oswalt, U.S. Air Force Spouse

there are different comfort levels between being stationed in Germany and in Georgia (the country, not the state).

Wherever you end up, realize it won't always be the dream assignment others imagine it to be. Everyday life with its daily aggravations will continue, just in a different time zone, even in coveted European assignments.

If you are stationed overseas, you should know that even though you are an American abroad, you will still need to be aware of and abide by the laws of the host nation you are stationed in. You also may have to learn how to correctly convert your dollars to some other currency. It wouldn't hurt to accept the reality that employment opportunities for you may be few and far between or simply nonexistent. If you have teenagers who want to work, know that the competition for positions at the local food court or commissary bagging lanes is intense.

Living conditions may also vary. You could potentially live off the military installation within the host nation itself, or you may be required to live in government housing on the military installation. Each has its pros and cons depending on the place.

Get off base. Learn some of the language. Enjoy the culture.

—Nick Johnson, U.S. Navy Sailor

Your service member spouse might also be very busy while you are posted overseas. Depending on what he does in the military, frequent deployments and TDYs/TADs may be a common reality. In other words, you have to be willing to get out there and do things in a foreign land all by yourself or with the new friends you make both on and off the base.

Being stationed overseas, however, can be a once (or twice) in a lifetime experience. As long as you realize and accept that things are often done differently than they are in the United States, you should be fine.

These additional tips may help you and your family to adjust to life overseas.

- Don't negatively compare life in your host nation country with the USA in a "that's not how we do it in the USA" kind of way. It won't win you any new friends, and it's considered rather rude.
- If you live and/or work on the military installation, don't stay there 24/7. Leave the base or post and make an effort to learn about your new community and its environs. That's where the adventure begins!
- Think hard before you move overseas without command sponsorship. Your access to the military installation and important services to include health care may be limited. You may also only be allowed to stay in the country for a limited period of time without it.
- Learn everything you can about your soon-to-be-home abroad before you get there. Joining community-specific online social media groups (i.e., Facebook) may be helpful unless they are full of trolls.
- Make a genuine attempt to learn the language of your host nation. A few words sincerely attempted can go a long way to making your life easier.
- Be street smart when you are out and about in a foreign country. The setting may be picture perfect, but the world can be a less than stable place as we know all too well from recent terrorist attacks. Don't let fear of what could happen stop you from experiencing an OCONUS assignment. At the same time, remain vigilant and don't bring unnecessary attention to yourself.

> If you are overseas, do not compare it to the States, especially when it comes to expecting people to speak English! That is the biggest mistake I saw while living overseas.
>
> —Nat Benipayo, U.S. Air Force Spouse (Retired)

- Be fully informed before you sign any contracts or enter into any legal agreements, verbal or written. In some places, verbal agreements are binding.
- Respect the customs and traditions of the host nation. It's the right thing to do whether you agree with them or not.
- Learn the correct number for emergency services where you are stationed. Hint: it's not 911.

- Don't travel anywhere without having your military ID card, U.S. passport, and SOFA stamp on you at all times.

Finally, when you are stationed overseas you assume the unofficial role as representative of the United States. Don't embarrass us. We pay our politicians good money to do that for us.

> Don't make other military-affiliated families and people your only social network. Especially when you live overseas, get out into the community and make outside friends.
>
> —Aubrey Kaufman, DoD Civilian Employee

UNACCOMPANIED TOURS: THE LONELY MOVE

In this chapter, we've gone into great detail regarding how to make the best of family PCS moves. You now have lots wise tips and tricks for comforting your kids, your dog, and even the movers.

You might need to know how to comfort yourself, too, as orders could one day arrive that don't include you or your family members on them. The only name on them is your uniformed spouse, and he or she is going solo for a year or more without you. This is called an unaccompanied tour, and it is no fun for anyone, or at least for you.

No one likes to be separated from a member of his close family, but this is a real possibility in military life. Each member of your family may handle this situation in a different way, of course.

As with a family move, make an effort to keep everyone informed on what is happening on an age-appropriate level. Stress that it is not forever but it will be for a given period of time, and everyone has to pull together to make it work.

Everyone should understand that it's okay to feel angry, frustrated, stressed out, or sad about the impending separation. These are all normal feelings. Accept them.

Talk together as a family and decide how you will effectively manage the separation. It may help to create some expectations.

For example, commit to checking in with each other on a weekly basis online or over the telephone if possible. Do your best to keep everyone connected even though the miles may separate you. Understand that every day won't be easy, but that this, too, shall pass.

For more tips on handling separations, see chapter 6, "Dealing with Deployments and Other Separations."

This lifestyle is not easy, and it has many road bumps for all members of the family. However, try to approach each assignment as an adventure. You may not always be thrilled with the location or the job, but each assignment is typically for a short period of time.

—Heather Robinson Unruh, U.S. Air Force Spouse

5

MILITARY SPOUSE CAREERS
AND EDUCATION

It's important to stay flexible, especially if you want a career of your own.

—Rebecca Roth, U.S. Air Force Spouse

If you want to work in a meaningful job or if you want to build a career, then you should be happy because today, more than ever before, those are viable possibilities despite the challenges that come with this military life.

There are also more opportunities open to you today to help you fund your college degree or become certified in a particular career field.

While the employment situation is still far from perfect, it *is* greatly improved. A big reason for this is the unprecedented collaborative efforts among government agencies, nonprofit organizations, and businesses.

Initiatives such as the Military Spouse Employment Partnership (MSEP) and Hiring Our Heroes (HOH) have helped many employers finally see the value in hiring and actually retaining mobile military spouses throughout PCS moves.

The DoD's Spouse Education and Career Opportunities (SECO) and the My Career Advancement Account (MyCAA) Scholarship program can be credited for making practical career education and free dollars for job training and state-specific licensure readily available to eligible military spouses.

Spouses who move because of their military orders and have to leave their jobs behind now also have better access to unemployment benefits in nearly all the states.

Organizations outside the DoD deserve much credit, too, as they have been instrumental in enhancing employment and education opportunities for military spouses through job placement, education, skills training, mentoring, career advocacy, and so much more.

They include such notables as:

- Blue Star Families (BSF), http://www.bluestarfamilies.org
- Business and Professional Women's Foundation (BPW), http://www.joiningforcesmentoringplus.org
- InGear Career, http://www.ingearcareer.org
- Military Spouse JD Network, http://www.msjdn.org
- Military Spouse Corporate Career Network (MSCCN), http://www.msccn.org
- National Military Family Association (NMFA), http://www.military families.org
- MilSpouse eMentor Program, https://ementorprogram.org
- MOAA Spouse, http://www.moaablogs.org

FIVE MILITARY SPOUSE EMPLOYMENT REALITIES

Even with so many benevolent groups working on our behalf, there are still certain realities of which you should be aware.

Reality #1: *There are still obstacles to employment, and some of them are big.*

Despite the many advances in this area, it can still be difficult to grow and maintain a career when you are married to someone in the military for any number of reasons.

- Frequent PCS moves sometimes make the hope of career continuity and advancement a joke.
- Your spouse works in a demanding job that, believe it or not now, can affect your professional life, too.
- Locational lack of affordable and/or reliable and convenient childcare hinders your efforts.
- Lengthy and costly state-to-state professional licensing requirements prevent you from working in your chosen career field.
- Some employers are still hesitant to hire spouses when they suspect they will eventually leave.
- Underemployment runs rampant. You might be able to find a job, but it may be one well beneath your skill set.

- Job opportunities may be limited wherever you happen to be stationed, making a consistent work history impossible.

Whatever reason sounds like yours, the result is often the same professional short end of the stick.

Reality #2: *You do have career choices.*

We don't always think we have choices when it comes to having a real career or keeping a good job, but we do. We just may not like the alternatives. They can be hard ones.

For example, if you happen to have a great job and PCS orders arrive theoretically sending you and your family off to a new duty station, you don't have to go with your spouse. You can stay put and continue to work in your career.

Many military families today make the decision to *geobach* (become a geographical bachelor) for the sake of their respective careers. Of course, the decision is a big one that could come with potentially difficult consequences as well.

You both have to be emotionally, financially, and physically able to maintain two households. You have to be committed to the idea, but it certainly can work if you want it bad enough.

Reality #3: *It helps to think outside your skill set.*

An open mind and a willingness to think outside your existing skill set will help you get hired faster as you move from place to place.

You may think of yourself as a [*insert your job title here*], but your duty station, the place you will call your home for the next two to three years, may not have any job openings for what you do.

When that happens (*not if, but when*), open your mind to other possibilities. Examine your skills in a new light and determine how they can be used in other kinds of positions that you may not have previously considered.

Not being able to find a job you are trained to do and want to do can be disappointing. At some point, however, you have to decide whether you will hold out for the perfect job that may never materialize or accept something else in the meantime.

There's not a lot of room for job snobbery, either, particularly if you are stationed someplace with limited job opportunities.

Reality #4: *It helps to be skilled in the art of finding a job.*

Job search skills are necessary and go far beyond having a decent resume. For example, you have to know how to network and know where to look for the potential jobs in your community. You have to be able to speak about yourself professionally to others you may or may not know in both informal situations and during job interviews. You have to understand how to establish a realistic salary range and negotiate for it and future benefits. You have to know how to use social media to your job search advantage, too.

If you don't have the job search skills you need, they can be learned, and they are readily available to you.

Visit the Employment Readiness Program at the family support center or access Military OneSource's Spouse Education and Career Opportunities (SECO) (http://www.militaryonesource.mil/education-and-employment/spouse-education-and-career-opportunities), or check out some of the other non-DoD employment resources noted at the beginning of this chapter.

Reality #5: *Your attitude is important.*

Your attitude can make or break your job prospects and/or your career. The situation may not be perfect, but how you choose to view it and confront the challenges will determine whether or not you succeed on a professional level and, frankly, on a personal one as well.

The sooner you accept that there is not a straight line to success, however you define it, the better. The journey to it can be a curvy and flowing line, sometimes jagged, painful, and even bittersweet. It can be one that travels all over the place. It is those unexpected side trips through employment peaks and valleys that often lead you to where you ultimately want to be or are meant to be in life.

> I have worked many different jobs that have nothing to do with my degree. Try to make the most out of the area you are stationed at.
>
> —Rebecca Roth, U.S. Air Force Spouse

HOW TO FIND A JOB AT YOUR NEW DUTY STATION

Finding a job when you have just arrived at a brand-new duty station or you are headed to one can be slightly overwhelming.

Unless the job market is flush with ample opportunity, expect finding a job to take some time. The average search can take three to six months, or even longer. You should have budgeted for this time. If you haven't, make sure you learn from that this time!

Whether jobs are plentiful or not may depend on where you are stationed and what you have to offer employers, but there are job possibilities if you know where to look.

If you aren't sure how to begin, then expand your local network by visiting or calling the employment readiness program manager at the military family center in the community where you want to work. The program manager or specialists there can help you identify specific leads in that community that you may not be aware of simply because you're new to it. They can also help you create or revise your resume and prepare for the job interview process.

It may be a good idea for spouses to begin searching and applying for jobs well before arrival. Consider both on- and off-installation options.

—Jennifer Oswalt, U.S. Air Force Spouse

Where the Jobs Are Located

Generally speaking, the following types of employment opportunities are typically found on or around a military community:

- federal job opportunities on the military installation
- state jobs within the local community
- defense contracting jobs both on and off the military installation
- private industry and nonprofit jobs in the local community
- freelance and self-employment job opportunities anywhere
- volunteer employment anywhere

How to Find Out About Specific Openings

You can find out about specific job openings, existing or potential, in a number of ways.

- Access the employer's website and look under Careers/Employment.
- Connect with the local chamber of commerce to learn about area employers.
- Network with people who work in your career field.
- Network with employees or friends who work where you want to work.

- Visit the Employment Readiness Program at the family support center.
- Access online job sites.
- Connect with others online through LinkedIn, Facebook, Twitter, and other sites.

Table 5.1.   Top Job Search Websites

Indeed	www.indeed.com
Monster	www.monster.com
Glassdoor	www.glassdoor.com
CareerBuilder	www.careerbuilder.com
SimplyHired	www.simplyhired.com
Aol Jobs	www.aoldjobs.com
JobDiagnosis	www.jobdiagnosis.com
Beyond	www.beyond.com
ZipRecruiter	www.ziprecruiter.com
USAJobs	www.usajobs.gov
Snagajob	www.snagajob.com
theLadders	www.theladders.com
Dice	www.dice.com
Salary	www.salary.com
Bright	www.bright.com

- Register with reputable staffing agencies or recruiters.

Table 5.2.   Top Five Largest U.S. Staffing Firms

Allegis Group	http://www.allegisgroup.com
Adecco	http://www.adecco.com
Randstad Holding	http://www.randstad.com
Manpower Group	http://www.manpower.com
Kelly Services	www.kellyservices.com

- Keep up with the local business news in your area (online or print).
- Take advantage of military spouse specific and related job sites.

Table 5.3.   Military Spouse and Related Job-Seeker Sites

Military Spouse Employment Partnership	https://msepjobs.militaryonesource.mil
Hiring Our Heroes	www.uschamberfoundation.org/hiring-our-heroes
National Military Spouse Network	http://www.nationalmilitaryspousenetwork.org
Military Spouse Business Association	https://milspousebiz.org
Blue Star Careers (Blue Star Families)	https://bluestarfam.org/resources/blue-star-careers

Military.com Spouse Employment	http://www.military.com/spouse/career-advancement
Military Spouse Corporate Career Network	http://www.msccn.org
National Military Spouse Network	http://www.nationalmilitaryspousenetwork.org
InGear Career	www.ingearcareer.org

Running a Smooth Job Search Campaign

Knowing where to look for the jobs is important, but there is more to finding a job than that.

- Be prepared for the job search. Have a good cover letter and resume ready to revise for each job opportunity you apply for. Know where to look for the jobs and how to interview successfully for them.
- Make sure the searchable online you that is in essence your online professional presence is marketable to potential employers.
- Make consistently looking for a job your job for the time being. You have to put in effort every day to make it happen.
- Volunteer selectively and meaningfully in the meantime. Choose where you volunteer your time and experience carefully. Ideally, it should be somewhere you hope to ultimately get hired. Yes, you may be working sans paycheck, but volunteering in this way will allow you to minimize resume gaps, network with others, and gain new skills. Some organizations provide free childcare for their volunteers, too. Read more about the pros and cons of Volunteering for the Greater Good later in this chapter.
- Create your own job opportunity. If you can't find a decent job, create one. Pitch the idea to an employer and just see where the proposal takes you.
- Enhance your skill set. If your skills aren't currently marketable, get new ones though formal or self-directed methods. Never stop learning.
- If you are a foreign-born spouse who wants to work for the U.S. government, consider obtaining U.S. citizenship so that more employment doors will be open for you. Obviously, this is a highly personal choice and shouldn't be made on the basis of employment alone; however, it is an option that others have used successfully in the past.

- If you work in a career that requires you to have state-specific licensing and/or certifications, proactively plan for your next PCS to minimize your career downtime. Find out what you need to know well in advance if at all possible and start the arduous process early.
- If you have small children at home and childcare would cost more than your anticipated salary, objectively weigh the pros/cons of being employed. Decide for yourself what will work. Maybe you drive on with working now or you don't. Maybe you find a middle ground that keeps you from going insane and still advances your career goals in some way.
- Online and off, networking plays an important role in your career. Refresh and step it up. Keep it up. Review your online profiles and update them. Contribute to group discussions. Meet someone for lunch.
- There will always be someone who seems to have it all professionally when you don't. While it's good to admire someone and appreciate what they've done, it's not so good to envy them. Ironically, looks can also be deceiving anyway. Instead, focus on your career and what it is you are trying to achieve.

> Get involved. Always strive to learn and remain educated. Learn new jobs and skills that will allow each of you to have lives.
>
> —Aubrey Kaufman, DoD Civilian Employee

- Take full advantage of the military and local employment resources available to you.
- Network routinely with others even after you get a job.
- Be open to accepting a job that may lead to a better job later.
- Be patient and don't give up.

LOOKING FOR A JOB WHILE STATIONED OVERSEAS

It's not easy to find a job in a world you are familiar with, and it can be more challenging to find one when you are stationed overseas or Outside the Continental United States (OCONUS). The good news here is that it is not impossible, either, if you know the deal ahead of time.

Whether you are job hunting in Germany, Japan, Bahrain, or anywhere else overseas, know the fine print before you arrive in the country.

It's going to take more time than you think it will to find a job. Even if you are PCSing to a large military community abroad that resembles little America, it could take three months or more to get hired. If you are moving somewhere smaller, it can take a year or more. If you are a family that depends on two paychecks and PCSing will take you down to one, be prepared financially for a long period of unemployment.

You may have a hard time finding out about available jobs. For one, they are not all advertised in one central location. They can be all over the place and hard to find.

OCONUS federal job opportunities (GS jobs and NAF positions) are easy to access at www.usajobs.gov. Federal jobs may not be the only game in town, though. There could be defense contracting and nonprofit positions in the military community and other jobs outside the main gate in the host nation community, even ones with American companies that operate abroad.

Job opportunities may be limited. If you are moving to a remote installation or being posted at an embassy, expect to find limited or even nonexistent job opportunities within the military community. A tour spent being unemployed can easily happen in such circumstances.

You may not be allowed to legally work off the military installation. Whether you are legally allowed to work in a job off the installation OCONUS depends on the unique Status of Forces Agreements (SOFA) between the host nation and the United States.

If you do get hired in the host nation, you will most likely need to have a working command of the local language and be required to pay host nation taxes in addition to U.S. federal taxes.

Don't accept a position working OCONUS until you are clear on your taxation requirements and your legality for doing so. Visit the installation legal office for clarification and read IRS Publication 54, Tax Guide for U.S. Citizens and Resident Aliens Abroad.

There are only so many jobs to go around. If your goal is to get a paycheck in short order, you can't be too picky in the process. There are a limited number of OCONUS jobs available on the installation and stiff competition for them among other family members, veterans, and tourists who would love to land an ID card to stay in the country for a few years.

It is easy to get discouraged while you're job hunting OCONUS. At times, it can feel like you will never get hired, and there's good reason for that feeling. You might not. You might also meet other spouses who have given up on their job searches altogether. You will also meet others who are professionally bitter and utterly convinced the system is rigged and only friends of friends get hired.

When you feel discouraged or when you meet others who have given up, you have to decide which road you're going to walk here, so to speak.

You can give up, too, and be bitter in the process. Don't be surprised if that apathy spreads to other areas of your life while you're living overseas. Or you can consistently and patiently continue to try to find a good job, or a decent one, and make it an effort to take cultural advantage of the short time you will be living overseas.

Self-employment may or may not be an option OCONUS. If you were already self-employed before you leave the United States, you may or may not be able to operate your business while you are OCONUS. It will depend on the type of business you have, where you want to operate it from, and the command and host nation climate for allowing it.

If you are allowed to own and operate your own business OCONUS, know that you are not permitted to use the military postal system, shopping venues, or government-registered vehicles for business purposes.

If you are planning to work from your military quarters, you will probably need installation commander approval first. Obtaining that will be a paperwork drill requiring layers of coordination between other installation authorities.

If you are planning to work from your rented home off the installation, you will most likely need to have permission from the local city government to do so, along with a business license.

You may not be allowed to work off base/post OCONUS. Whether or not you can work off the military installation within the host nation will depend on the Status of Forces Agreement (SOFA) between the United States and the host nation you are stationed in. Every country has its own set of rules concerning the employment of U.S. forces and their family members.

For example, in Germany you are permitted to work outside the gate, but you must pay German taxes in the process. In Spain, you are not allowed to work within the host nation at all.

Here are a few more tips to help you find and keep a job while you are stationed overseas:

- Research the community before you get there using the DoD Military Installations Guide and contact the employment readiness program manager at the family support center. On-installation employment options usually include: appropriated federal employment (GS jobs); nonappropriated (NAF) federal employment (MWR jobs); defense contracting (mission-related and community services); and nonprofit (USO, Red Cross) jobs.

- You may be eligible to use Military Spouse Preference in Employment as you apply for federal jobs. Know what this is and how you can take advantage of it. See Working for Uncle Sam later in this chapter for more information.

- If you are job hunting within a joint command community (also often referred to as a *purple* community), consider job opportunities across the Services. In theory, all federal job vacancies should be posted on USAJobs, but it doesn't hurt to check the individual service employment sites as well.

Table 5.4.   Individual Service Branch Federal Job Sites

Army Civilian Service	https://armycivilianservice.usajobs.gov/
Air Force Civilian Employment	https://airforce.usajobs.gov/
Navy and Marine Corps Jobs	https://don.usajobs.gov/
Coast Guard	http://www.uscg.mil/civilian/careeropps.asp

- *Plan to spend your unemployed time wisely.* Volunteer meaningfully. Consider going back to college or earning a specific license or certification instead. Investigate the possibilities of working online.

VOLUNTEERING FOR THE GREATER GOOD

There is nothing like feeling that you are part of something bigger than yourself.

By making a difference, you are building a better community for yourself and your family members.

—Carmen Carlisle, U.S. Marine Corps Spouse

Volunteering is always a great idea for both professional and personal reasons. When you are trying to find a job, volunteering can be the key to your ultimate success.

If "no one else" will do it, perhaps it's time to consider that it is something that is no longer needed or valued. Volunteer projects should bless BOTH the volunteer and the community.

—Stephanie Hodges, U.S. Navy Spouse (Retired)

Too often, we think that those experiences somehow don't count because we didn't receive a paycheck for doing them. When we think like that, we are shortchanging ourselves in a big way. We aren't seeing the big and important picture.

Volunteerism matters, not only on an intrinsic level but on a career-enhancing level, too. Consider the many advantages involved:

- Volunteering gives you the chance to become familiar with your new community while giving you the chance to meet new friends.
- It allows you to keep your skills current and learn new ones as well.
- It decreases the frequency of employment gaps on your resume.
- Volunteering gives you the chance to try a new job or career on for size before you commit to it.
- It gives you the priceless opportunity to network with others in your community who may be able to help you land a paying job.
- It potentially positions you as the best candidate for the next open paid position within the organization that you're serving.
- It's good for your health and your social life.

Get involved in your new community. Volunteering not only gives you the opportunity to meet new people and build lasting friendships, it benefits your professional resume and can also open the door to a new job.

—Carmen Carlisle, U.S. Marine Corps Spouse

Putting Volunteer Work on Your Resume

Whether you're professionally motivated or not, you may have many occasions to volunteer within the military community. If you do so, make sure you give yourself the relevant credit you deserve for those experiences on your resume.

There are so many volunteer opportunities not only on the military installation, but also in the community. Not only is this a good way to meet other
people, but it can help you network if you are looking for a job.

—Rebecca Roth, U.S. Air Force Spouse

How? It's easy. First, figure out whether or not there is a direct skills
relationship between your volunteer job and the type of job you wish to
land.

If there is and you have a consistent volunteer work history, then treat
that volunteer experience just as you would a paying job. Give it the space
it deserves as another job on your resume.

Omit the use of the word *volunteer* in the job title. Use an appropriate
position title and provide an accomplishments-based description as your
work narrative.

Many organizations have established job titles and descriptions for
their unique volunteer positions. If you are having difficulty figuring out
what yours is, talk to the supervisor or manager where you volunteer and
ask for some guidance.

Highlight those skills that best support the objective of your resume.
Quantify your accomplishments and responsibilities, just as you would any
paying position.

For example, if you were the chairperson of a membership committee
for an organization, note the number of volunteers you supervised. Plug in
the amount of membership dollars that were raised under your stewardship.
Mention your leadership in event planning and program implementation.

If, on the other hand, your volunteer work experience does not support the type of job you are seeking, then you may need to take a different
approach to highlighting the information on your resume.

Instead of treating the unrelated volunteer experience as you would a
paying job, consider adding it elsewhere on your resume in a separate section titled Community Service.

Is that experience one that will mean something to a potential employer? If the answer is yes, then don't bury it at the end of your resume
or exclude it. If the answer is no, then consider whether it truly belongs
on it in the first place.

If the volunteer experience involves religious or political activities and
you choose to include it on your resume, be certain to keep the content

focused on the skills you used and not on your own personal beliefs. Keep in mind that not everyone shares your views. Some employers, like it or not, may come to snap judgments based on their own beliefs that could negatively affect your chances of landing an interview.

When you are finished adding your volunteer work experience to your resume, get someone else to look it over for you.

From commands, schools, church, spouse groups, military focus groups, and various other organizations, there are many opportunities to offer help to your community, but no one should spread themselves thin and subsequently stress themselves and their families by overvolunteering.

—Stephanie Hodges, U.S. Navy Spouse (Retired)

Where You Can Find Volunteer Opportunities

You can find volunteer opportunities in many places, wherever you are stationed. If you aren't sure where to begin your search, visit your installation's volunteer coordinator at the family support center.

Be okay with saying "no." At many times, you will have a lot more on your plate than someone rooted in a hometown. You may not have as much to give right now, and that is okay. Family is first.

—Siggi, U.S. Air Force Spouse

Other organizations that can help match you with opportunities include the following:

Table 5.5.   Volunteer Websites

United We Serve	http://www.serve.gov
Combined Federal Campaign (CFC) Today	http://www.cfctoday.org
Charity Navigator	http://www.charitynavigator.org
VolunteerMatch	http://www.volunteermatch.org
World Volunteer Web	http://www.worldvolunteerweb.org
Idealist.org	http://www.idealist.org
Charity Navigator	www.charitynavigator.org

Learn how to ask for time to think about and consult your family about a possible venture before committing. "No, it just doesn't work for me/us right now" is a perfectly acceptable reply after careful consideration. It makes saying "yes" to the right project even sweeter!

—Stephanie Hodges, U.S. Navy Spouse (Retired)

WORKING FOR UNCLE SAM

You might think that federal employment would be the path to career continuity and success for your mobile lifestyle. You might be right, too. You should also know that having a federal job at one duty station doesn't necessarily mean you will easily land one at the next duty station. That would make entirely too much sense.

Both getting your foot in the federal government and keeping it there requires eternal patience, current knowledge about the hiring process, and just plain old good luck.

Military Spouse Preference for Employment

If you are a military spouse and are included on the official orders, then you may be eligible to use military spouse preference for employment purposes.

The Military Spouse Preference Program, established under the Military Family Act of 1985, offers employment placement preference in DoD civilian personnel positions to military spouses who meet certain criteria.

The program applies to DoD vacancies only, meaning that MSP isn't available in other government agencies such as the Department of Justice or the Bureau of Land Management.

Of course, there are also variations to the program and exceptions that allow local hiring authorities to tailor their policies to meet their requirements, often leading to the infamous "it's who you know" syndrome.

To be eligible for the MSP, you should:

- Be the spouse of an active duty member of the U.S. Military Services, including the Coast Guard or full-time National Guard

- Be relocating (not for separation or retirement) to accompany your military sponsor under a permanent change of station (PCS) move to an active duty assignment; you may apply for MSP as early as thirty days prior to your reporting date at the new duty station. If you are moving overseas, however, you may have to actually be in the country before you can use it. Contact the Civilian Personnel Advisory Center (CPAC) where you are headed for more information.
- Have been married to the military sponsor prior to the sponsor's reporting date at the new assignment
- Apply for a position within commuting distance of the sponsor's permanent new duty station. Contact the hiring CPAC to determine what "commuting distance" really means. In Germany, for example, it may mean the entire country if you're willing to drive across it every day for your job.
- Rank among the "best qualified" candidates for the position. That's right. You still have to be the right person for the job anyway.

The MSP program allows military spouses to receive preference over other candidates; however, some individuals are given a higher preference status over them, too.

Disabled veterans, employees registered in the Equal Employment Opportunity (EEO) program, and former employees returning from overseas are among those given higher preference than military spouses.

MSP applies to two main types of federal employment within the DoD: civil service or appropriated fund (AF), and nonappropriated fund (NAF).

They are considered separate hiring authorities and generally have separate hiring offices on military installations.

Even within the military spouse preference program, there are various specific hiring authorities that may or may not apply to it, depending on your circumstances. Let's look at a couple below.

Executive Order 13473

You may be eligible for hiring under Executive Order 13473 if you are a spouse of a member of the Armed Forces serving on active duty who has permanent change of station (PCS) orders (not for training).

This preference is limited to a maximum of two years from the date of the orders for the PCS and also limited to the geographic area as specified in the PCS orders.

To be eligible to use this authority:

- the spouse must relocate with the service member to be eligible or
- be the spouse of a 100 percent disabled service member injured while on active duty or
- be the unremarried widow or widower of a service member who was killed while performing active duty

Note the Office of Personnel Management (OPM) eliminated the two-year eligibility limitation to provide spouses of certain deceased or 100 percent disabled veterans with unlimited eligibility for noncompetitive appointment effective September 30, 2011.

Overseas Military Spouse Preference

You are eligible for this hiring category if you are the spouse of an active duty U.S. Armed Forces service member and:

- you and the sponsor were married prior to the relocation (before the PCS move)
- you have arrived at the overseas duty station identified on the PCS orders
- since the relocation, you have not accepted or declined a permanent position at the new duty station of the sponsor
- you are among the best qualified

This overseas preference can be granted only once per PCS relocation. Once you accept or decline a position, either appropriated fund (AF) or nonappropriated fund (NAF) at the new duty station, your eligibility for preference terminates whether or not preference was applied.

Executive Order 12721

This is an EO available to those returning from an OCONUS tour. If you have completed fifty-two weeks of service or 2,087 hours in certain position(s) performed under a local hire appointment(s) overseas, then you may be eligible for this hiring authority. The work must be performed during the time the family member was accompanying a sponsor officially assigned to an overseas post and the family member must have received a fully successful or better (or equivalent) performance rating.

An individual must have been a family member at the time she or he met the overseas service requirement but does not need to be a family member at the time of noncompetitive appointment in the United States. A family member is a spouse or unmarried child under the age of twenty-three. Any law, Executive Order, or regulation that disqualifies an applicant for appointment in the competitive service also disqualifies the applicant for appointment under EO 12721.

Getting Started with the USAJobs Website

You apply for federal employment, AF and NAF positions, using the USAJobs.gov website.

Before you can apply for jobs, however, you have to a) create an account in USAJobs first and b) understand how to read a job vacancy announcement before you waste your valuable time.

Step by Step: Creating an Account in USAJobs

1. Access www.usajobs.gov. On the top right-hand side of the page, you see the option to either Sign In or Create an Account. Click Create an Account.
2. Enter your primary email address and create a user name. Agree to their terms and then follow the prompts to create your account. Write down your user name. You will need it again later, and you will forget it if you don't.
3. You will be sent an email to the primary email address. You'll need to access this in order to fully establish your account. You can only use one account per email address.
4. Establish your password and provide answers to your security questions.
5. Finally, you can access your account and begin to create your profile.
6. Click Edit Profile and do just that. You'll enter your mailing address and telephone number. On the next screen, you'll indicate your hiring preferences. Click Military Spouse and any others that might apply to you.
7. On the next screen, you'll indicate whether you are willing to travel or not and what type of jobs you will consider. Pay attention to what you enter under the type of work and what type of work schedule sections of the profile input. For example, if you note that

you will only consider permanent employment and then you later apply for a temporary job lasting more than year, you won't be considered for the job because your profile and the job you actually applied for don't match. Make things match. Or select (and mean) *all* on the profile options page.

8. After entering this information, you will be queried regarding your notification settings. Pick whatever appeals to you at this point and then click Finish.

9. Back at the main account screen, you have the option to upload or create up to five federal resumes. More on federal resumes below; however, suffice it say right now that any resume you upload or create should be specifically targeted to a unique job or type of job.

10. At the main account screen, you also have the option to create up to ten job searches. For example, you are stationed in Colorado Springs and you only want to have job openings in Colorado Springs sent directly to your email address. You can make this happen, with or without further parameters.

11. You'll also notice an Inbox on your main account screen. If USA-Jobs ever wants to let you know about something, you'll see that you have mail in your inbox.

12. When you are actually browsing the USAJobs site, you can click the option of Save Job and it will be saved to your unique account, assuming you remember and can supply your login credentials.

13. Under the Saved Documents section of USAJobs, you can upload and maintain up to ten documents. Tip: While you may not know exactly what jobs you will be applying for at this point, you can still upload some of the commonly requested pieces of supporting documentation, such as your college transcript, a copy of military orders showing you as the spouse (if you are claiming MSP), a DD 214 (if you have prior military service), and more.

14. The Application Status section of the account dashboard will show you—you guessed it—the status of your job applications. It will tell you if you have completed an application and if your application has been reviewed, selected for referral, or whatever the case may be. Bear in mind that not all statuses are updated on a routine basis, however, by staffing specialists who are working a specific hiring action. Keep in mind that the website is constantly evolving. This means that today's directions may differ from tomorrow's. Always read what is in front of you and follow the directions.

Now you're ready to begin searching for jobs.

Important: Before you begin your search for jobs on the USAJobs site, be sure you click on Federal Employees on the first screen underneath the keyword and location search boxes. Many job seekers neglect to do this because they think it means that they have to already be a federal employee. You don't. You have to be eligible for federal employment, and with MSP, prior military service, or past federal employment, you are. Not clicking this will result in far fewer potential jobs for which you can or might wish to apply for.

Identifying and Applying for Federal Job Opportunities

Job vacancy announcements on USAJobs are written in English, so you'd think it would be easy to understand; however, they can be confusing if you aren't sure what to pay specific attention to.

Let's assume for the moment that you have identified a job you're interested in and you think you want to apply for it.

Before you spend hours and hours targeting your federal resume to that job (which is something you'll want to do if you want to be competitive for it), first make sure you are actually eligible to apply for it in the first place.

You can determine whether you can apply for the job by glancing at the WHO MAY APPLY section of the job vacancy announcement.

Ironically, the WHO MAY APPLY section might clearly state who can apply or not. It might say something like "Status Candidates." You, dearest job seeker, may or may not be a status candidate. Before you rule yourself out, read a little further down in the announcement to a second section also titled WHO MAY APPLY, which will tell you for sure.

If you are eligible to apply, great, but don't start working on your resume yet.

Instead, read over the rest of the job vacancy announcement to be sure, in your gut, that you are indeed a potential candidate.

Pay specific attention to the DUTIES, KEY REQUIREMENTS, and QUALIFICATIONS sections. Click on the VIEW OCCUPATIONAL QUESTIONNAIRE link as well and read over the skills assessment questions.

If you feel that you are a match based on that information and you would be able to fully support the skills within the scope of a federal resume in great detail, then actually apply for the job.

Read and follow the directions provided within the announcement carefully. Too many times, ambitious, confident, and highly qualified job seekers neglect to do this. The end result is that they are eliminated from consideration for employment over a minor administrative error that could have been easily prevented.

Don't be that job seeker.

If you do want to land a federal job, then routinely stay on top of new openings and apply for positions promptly. In an apparent effort to limit the overwhelming number of applications, some vacancy announcements now state that officials will accept resumes through the closing date *or* until the first fifty, two hundred, or some other magical cutoff number of applications are received.

While great reforms have been made in the hiring process over the years, the amount of effort and patience required on your part to actually secure a federal job is nothing short of monumental.

The average job search can take three months to a year, depending on where you are applying and the type of jobs they have available.

For more detailed assistance in getting hired by the federal government, visit the employment readiness program manager at the family service center on the military installation.

BECOMING YOUR OWN BOSS

The constant career starts and stops that we are prone to experience in the military lifestyle can be frustrating and stressful over the course of time. One way to avoid such angst is to become self-employed. Many spouses today have successfully chosen this route. If you have a marketable skill, it just might be the answer to your job search challenges, too.

The advantages to being self-employed are tempting:

- As the boss, you determine your own working hours and priorities.
- If your business is service oriented and/or online, it may PCS easily with you.
- You may actually spend less on childcare, clothing, dry cleaning, and transportation.
- There could be federal and state tax advantages as a result of being self-employed.
- You have increased flexibility to think outside the box.

There are potential disadvantages as well:

- It's all on you. You are responsible for your success or lack thereof.
- Paychecks may not be regular or even forthcoming for some time.
- You get to pay the bills of the business to include federal and state taxes.
- You may work far more than the standard forty-hour workweek.
- It can be hard to successfully balance your home and work life.

If you think self-employment might be a good career move for you, then do your homework first before you buy those cute business cards.

- Visit your on-installation employment readiness office to see if they offer classes on how to start your own business.
- Access the many resources of the Small Business Administration online at http://www.sba.gov. They are the experts in showing you how to start a business and how to secure funding for it.
- Become a member of the local chamber of commerce and volunteer if possible with them. It is an open door to an instant network of supporters and potential customers.
- Maintain your online presence. Update your online social and professional networking links announcing your new business when the time is right. If marketing isn't your favorite thing to do, hire someone to do it for you. There are lots of talented fellow military spouses out there available to assist.
- Network with military spouses and others who have done the same thing to learn from them. You can do that easily online through organizations such as the National Military Spouse Network (http://www.nationalmilitaryspousenetwork.org/), the Military Spouse Business Association (http://milspousebiz.org/), and the National Association for the Self-Employed (http://www.nase.org), and Joining Forces Mentoring Plus (http://www.joiningforcesmentoring plus.org).

More Tips for Self-Employment Success

- Make your business a legal one. Research and obtain the requisite state licenses and permissions. You can find out information about doing so on the SBA site (http://www.sba.gov).

- Create a solid business plan.
- Be qualified for the business you want to call your own.
- Be financially prepared to become a one-paycheck family for a while.
- If you have a day job, don't quit it just yet. Consider launching your venture part time on the side until the business is strong enough to become a full-time job.
- Continue to foster your own professional development.
- Make sure your family understands and supports your efforts.
- If you live on a military installation, get permission from the installation commander to operate a business out of your quarters.
- If you are stationed overseas, don't use the military post office or your military registered car for business purposes. You may also have other U.S. and host nation restrictions or requirements depending on which country you are stationed in.

THE GRACEFUL EXIT: LEAVING YOUR JOB

What goes up, must come down, right? Sooner or later, you will find yourself having to leave a job for any number of potential reasons.

If career progression and continuity are your goals, then ideally you don't want to leave one job until you are certain you have another one waiting for you.

The ideal doesn't always happen. Life, however, does.

Military orders send you elsewhere. You can't stand your boss. Your family needs more of your time than your work is allowing you to give them. Your co-workers annoy you and you just can't deal with them any longer. You are underappreciated and underemployed. You don't like what you do. You just want a break. They don't pay you enough for what you have to put up with. You're bored.

Everybody has his own reasons for leaving a job.

Knowing how to gracefully leave a job, however, is nearly as important as knowing how to successfully land one.

If at all possible, you want to leave a job on a good note. You want people to remember you as being a professional.

The truth is that the military community can seem quite small at times. You might easily end up working with the same people again, or people who know them well and have talked about you.

Timing of your departure is key.

Once you have made the decision in your mind and in your heart to leave your employer, you should begin the planning of your actual exit.

Don't make the mistake of sharing your news with your co-workers before you share it with your supervisor. You want to control the information flow here so that a graceful exit is possible.

Look at a calendar and determine when your last working day will be. Make sure you build in enough time to give the employer a chance to digest this news and start the succession planning process.

Be certain to examine and meet your own needs here as well. It's easy to forget that you have them if you are worried about inconveniencing someone else.

For example, you may not want to be working while you'll be busy trying to get things in your life ready to PCS, if that's the reason for your departure. Or you may need to work right up to a certain date in order to benefit from continued pay.

At a minimum, give your employer a two-week notice verbally and in writing. In some organizations, such as the federal government, that won't be enough time to recruit and hire a replacement. If you have the flexibility to offer up a longer notice, do so.

Your employer may be understanding of your decision, or he may not be. A lot will depend on your relationship with your boss and the reasons for your departure.

Be professional and as cooperative as possible. If you are able to assist in securing a replacement for your job, do so.

Don't leave a mess behind. Try to tie up any workload loose ends so those left behind can have an easier time doing your job after you're gone.

Talk to your human resources specialist and be sure you understand what happens to any of your benefits as you transition out of the job.

When There's Bad Blood

Not every goodbye is a good one.

If your employer or your co-workers are not understanding of your decision to leave, then there isn't a whole lot you can do about it unless they are being discriminatory or acting illegally toward you.

The best you can do when drama is involved is to minimize the damage and potentially speed up the timeline of departure.

Whatever you do, don't contribute to the dramatics. You have your reasons for leaving, and they are good ones.

If the employer, for whatever reason he thinks he has, can't accept your professional decision and you haven't given him reason for acting that way, then maybe parting isn't such sweet sorrow. Maybe it's a good thing for everyone.

FUNDING YOUR EDUCATION AND JOB TRAINING

Earning a college degree or obtaining a professional certification to help you advance in your career is expensive. According to Collegeboard.com, the average tuition and fees for one year of out-of-state college in 2016 is $23,893. Multiply that times four years and you get a cost of $95,572 for a four-year degree. That doesn't even include the cost of textbooks, and it assumes your room and board is the comfort of your own humble home.

While the cost is breathtaking (and retirement deterring, but I digress), you shouldn't let the high cost stand in your way of moving forward, as-suming forward is where you can professionally go with the experience.

In addition to the potential federal loans, grants, and scholarships of the usual variety, there are a number of military spouse specific programs and scholarships that can help you pay the tuition bills.

In-State Tuition Rates

You're going to like this.

According to the Higher Education Opportunity Act (H.R. 4137), under section 135, and which was signed into law on August 14, 2008, and extended the Higher Education Act of 1965 (HEA), spouses of mili-tary service members who are on active duty for more than thirty days are eligible to receive in-state tuition at public colleges and universities in the state where they reside or are permanently stationed.

Once enrolled and paying that in-state tuition, spouses are allowed to continue to pay it as long as you remain continuously enrolled at that institution, even if your service member is reassigned out of state.

Transfer of Post-9/11 GI Bill

If your uniformed spouse has unused Post-9/11 GI Bill educational benefits that he or she doesn't want to use, then all thirty-six months of those benefits may be eligible for transferability to you, one or more of your children, or any combination of spouse and child.

Whoever your uniformed spouse is willing to transfer the entitlement to must be enrolled in DEERS and be eligible for the benefits at the time of transfer in order to receive them.

Service members having this option must:

- have at least six years of service in the armed forces on the date of approval
- agree to serve four more additional years in the armed forces from the date of the election
- have at least ten years of service in the military (active duty and/or Selected Reserve) on the date of approval and be precluded from either standard policy or statute from committing four additional years of service and agree to serve for the maximum amount of time allowed
- be or become retirement eligible and agree to serve four additional years of service
- request the transfer of benefit and have it approved while in the armed forces

You can quickly see that there is quite a bit involved here, and this doesn't even cover all of it. Also, not to be pessimistic, but in our current cost-cutting-to-the-bone defense environment, don't be surprised if the benefit itself changes again in the future. Use it if you can, while you can. You can learn more about the Post-9/11 GI Bill transferability by contacting the education center on the military installation or by visiting http://www.benefits.va.gov/gibill/post911_gibill.asp.

My Career Advancement Account (MyCAA)

MyCAA is workforce-development program that provides eligible spouses with up to $4,000 of tuition assistance. The scholarship helps military spouses pursue licenses, certificates, certifications, or associate degrees necessary to gain employment in high-demand, high-growth, portable career fields.

You may be eligible for MyCAA if you are a spouse of a service member on active duty in pay grades E-1 to E-5, W-1 to W-2, and O-1 to O-2 and who can start and complete the coursework while the military spouse is on Title 10 military orders. National Guard and reserve component spouses in the same pay grades are also eligible.

If you are eligible to take advantage of this wonderful program, do so. It probably won't survive in the years to come due to budget cuts.

Scholarships and Grants

If you're seriously trying to save money on tuition bills, then scholarships and grants that you don't have to pay back should be on your short list of funding ideas.

Scholarship and grants are awarded based on varying criteria. Some of them are open to you simply because you are a military spouse.

As you might imagine, just because it is free money doesn't mean it is freely given to you without significant effort on your part. You have to tediously apply for scholarships and grants, and you won't be the only one doing so.

You can find scholarships and grants through federal and state government agencies, your college or university of choice, nonprofit and private organizations, and some employers. You'll find some of those organizations within our own military community.

Applying for Scholarships and Grants

- Read application directions and then follow them. Don't apply for opportunities that you aren't eligible for in the first place.
- Keep track of applications on a spreadsheet or similar document that includes the scholarship or grant name, sponsoring organization, contact information, web address, deadline date, award amount, criteria, required documents, and important deadline dates.
- Don't fall for scholarship scams. There are many telltale signs of fake scholarships to include application fees, loan fees, claims of guaranteed winnings, and unlimited eligibility.

Identifying Scholarships and Grants

There are a number of ways you can identify potential scholarships and grants. There are several major search engines to include:

- Big Future, http://bigfuture.collegeboard.org/
- College Data, http://www.collegedata.com
- CollegeNet, www.collegenet.com

- Fastweb, http://www.fastweb.comScholarships, http://www
.scholarships.com
- Scholarship Monkey, http://www.scholarshipmonkey.com

You can also find great information in these books:

- Gen Tanabe and Kelly Tanabe, *The Ultimate Scholarship Book 2016*
- *Scholarships, Grants & Prizes 2016* (Peterson's)
- Gen Tanabe and Kelly Tanabe, *1001 Ways to Pay for College*

Military-Related Scholarships and Grants

There are also many military-related scholarships and grants that you may be eligible to apply for. The following list of organizations is not all-inclusive, but it will certainly give you a good start:

Air Force Aid Society Education Grant Program
Air Force Aid Society General Henry H. Arnold Education Grant
    Program
Air Force Association
Armed Forces Communications and Electronics Associations (AF-
    CEA)
Army Emergency Relief (Spouse Educational Assistance Program)
Bryant & Stratton Salute to Spouses
Clovis Community College Military Spouse Scholarship
Coast Guard Foundation
Coast Guard Mutual Assistance (CGMA)
Commissioned Officers Foundation Scholarship
Corvias Foundation
Council of College and Military Educators Scholarships
Fisher House Foundation Scholarships
Folds of Honor Foundation
FRA Scholarship Program
Hope for the Warriors
Joanne Holbrook Patton Military Spouse Scholarship
Ladies Auxiliary of the FRA Scholarship
The Military Order of the Purple Heart
Military Service Recognition Scholarship
MOAA Educational Assistance
National Military Family Association

The Navy Marine Corps Relief Society (NMCRS)
Navy SEAL Foundation Scholarships
Navy Supply Corps Foundation Scholarships
NIWH Military Spouse Scholarship Program
Pat Tillman Scholars
Salute to Spouses
ThanksUSA Scholarship Program
U.S. Army Warrant Officers Association Scholarships
U.S. Coast Guard Work-Life Scholarships
VA Mortgage Center
Wings Over America Scholarship Foundation

In trying to secure funding for your education or training, don't forget these resources, either:

- admissions officer of the school you plan to attend
- community spouses club on your nearest military installation
- Department of Education for the state in which you reside and/or wish to attend school

6

DEALING WITH DEPLOYMENTS AND OTHER SEPARATIONS

There is no way to sugarcoat it, but deployments have become a reality in the military.

—Rebecca Roth, U.S. Air Force Spouse

No one looks forward to tearful goodbyes, but they are a real and often-repeated part of military family life.

When duty calls (and trust me on this one, duty never forgets your telephone number), your uniformed spouse has to go wherever the job sends him, whether you like it or not.

- He may be deployed to a scary place far, far away.
- She may have to go TDY/TAD (on temporary duty) somewhere else in the world.
- He may have to attend mandatory training.
- She may have to participate in a major exercise or training event.

Or, maybe your hard-working spouse isn't going anywhere requiring a packed bag. He just isn't coming home in time for dinner anytime soon on a regular basis.

When he does finally drag himself through the front door, his body may be present but his mind may be back on the job.

Separations of all kinds are simply business as usual in this world.

Taking Care of Business

In the last decade or so, military families have had lots of practice saying goodbye to their uniformed spouses who were being deployed, not just once, but multiple times.

It's hard enough dealing with one deployment. Dealing with multiple, one right after the other? Let's just say it can take a real toll on the service member, the family, and that whole concept of mission readiness.

To fully understand that toll and to minimize its damage, much research has been done through the years to figure out exactly what happens during a deployment. The goal of this research was to assist service members and their families in better navigating the periods of time leading up to, during, and after deployments.

The research has also enabled the DoD to better customize programs and services in support of its valued force and its equally valued families.

As a new military family member, it will help you to know about the stages of deployment now so that when you experience it, you and your family will be more prepared to get through it.

When will you go through this? *No one knows.*

Whenever it happens, your stages and the ones of the universally accepted deployment model may resemble one another or not. A lot will depend on the individuals involved, the units and its leadership, and the mission to be accomplished.

Regardless of all those not-so-minor details, it is a good idea to learn now about the cycles of deployment rather than to be emotionally sideswiped later.

Essentially, these are the phases of life you and your family will go through: predeployment, deployment, demobilization, and postdeployment/reintegration, and reunion.

PREDEPLOYMENT: PREPARING FOR THE INEVITABLE

When you first learn about the deployment, denial may be your best friend. Eventually, however, you start to mentally imagine what it will be like to live without your spouse for a long period of time. If you feel confused, stressed, resentful, or depressed, it's okay. Those emotions are to be expected. Tears are common, too.

Rest assured, there is a lot of uncertainty at this stage for everyone involved. Even your spouse may not know exactly when he'll be leaving.

As the deployment draws nearer, you may find that you both enter a Twilight Zone existence of sorts. It is that space in between the time before he leaves and the time he actually goes. He may be physically present, but the best part of him has already left the building. Many spouses say this is the worst part of all. I agree.

During this high-stress time, he may be worried about leaving you behind while he's busy trying to pack too many things in too few bags. He's required to attend briefing after briefing and do 1,001 other things the military tells him to do before he deploys.

He may be sad, anxious, and stressed all at the same time. A tiny part of him may be secretly thrilled professionally, but you're not indulging any of that emotion at this moment. No way. You are too busy being sad, anxious, and stressed all at the same time yourself. The kids, if you have them, are going through their own feelings, too. Even the dog may sense that something is up.

Tempers may flare amid this array of mixed feelings. Words may be said that are later regretted. You love your service member with all your heart, but if he asks you one more time where you moved something he desperately needs that you didn't touch in the first place, you just might lose it.

Perhaps, you think, it would just be in everybody's best interest to get this show on the road so it can one day end and life can theoretically go back to normal. (Normal, however, is just an illusion, but more on that later.) You both may begin to feel detached or withdrawn from one another as you each begin to shift life gears mentally. He may begin to focus more on the mission and less on you and your family.

Being a military family during deployment is easy . . . said no one ever.

The week before a deployment is THE WORST. It is a total emotional rollercoaster. Expect this and just ride it out.

—Kristin M. Sells, U.S. Air Force Brat, U.S. Army Spouse (Retired)

Before you exit the predeployment phase, you want to make sure you have your affairs in order.

- Make a genuine effort to be nice to each other and spend some quality time with one another. Deployments aren't easy for anyone. Do your best to make your last days together full of good memories.
- Try to connect to one another emotionally. Be clear with one another and know where you stand with each other.
- Prepare for the separation financially. Consider creating a deployment budget. At the very least, agree upon how the cash flow will be handled while you may be incommunicado with one another. Who will be responsible for making sure the bills are paid on time? How will you divide up the paychecks while he's gone? Do you have an emergency fund available to you should you need it? Do you both agree on what constitutes an emergency for tapping into it? Have this discussion well before the night before he leaves.
- Know where important documents are located before he leaves, too. Where is his will? Where are the vehicle loan papers and the tax-related documents?
- Discuss and determine how you will try to realistically keep in touch while you are separated. He may not know if he will even have Internet or telephone access at this point, but do your best to identify some possible means of keeping in touch.
- Arrange to have a power of attorney in place in case you need it to take care of legal matters in his absence, such as re-registering your car or paying your federal and/or state taxes. Have multiple copies of it, and keep it in a safe place.
- Get together a list of sources of support and various repair services to call in the event something falls apart in his absence because you can be certain something will fall apart in his absence and you will need to get it fixed.
- Make it a point to meet your neighbors if you don't already know them. If they are trustworthy, add them to your "call in case of an emergency" list.
- Make sure everyone in the house who is eligible for it has a current military ID card. If it will potentially expire during the separation, know how to get it renewed solo before you are solo. While you're at it, make sure everyone's information is updated in DEERS.
- Attend unit predeployment mobilization meetings and take good notes.
- Know the exact name of your service member's unit and how to contact the rear detachment in the event of a real emergency.

- Have multiple copies of your spouse's deployment orders on file.
- Don't share information about the impending deployment online or off with others who don't need to know details. It's a safety precaution for everyone involved.

Deployments are not easy. You will miss and worry about your spouse like crazy. This is where making friends and a strong support network helps get you through deployments. Establishing a routine and staying busy also helps during a deployment. Try not to compare what your spouse is doing with other spouses in the military. They can be in the same unit, but having to do totally different things.

—Rebecca Roth, U.S. Air Force Spouse

DEPLOYMENT: WHEN IT REALLY HAPPENS

In this phase, your serving spouse is deployed and off taking care of the mission wherever that mission happens to be located.

You may hear from him regularly, or not at all. It may help you to keep a journal or a running log of things you want to tell him while they are on your mind.

This is also a big adjustment time for you and your family as you begin to get used to everyday life sans your soldier, sailor, airman, or marine.

- Nurture your relationship through the miles. If your conversations are sporadic, it may help to write down daily events that you want to share with him. That way, when you do get to connect, you'll remember those things.
- Plan to keep long-distance communications on a positive note. Doing so will keep your spouse from being distracted from his potentially dangerous job. It may help to talk about things you will do together in the future, too, giving you both something to look forward to after the separation.
- You can let your spouse know you're thinking of him by putting together care packages for him and even for those deployed with him. Be creative, but keep it culturally appropriate so there aren't any issues when the box is opened.

> TDY, deployments, long hours, and usually no family nearby means it's up to the one at home to keep things running.
>
> —Jessica Leia Moss, U.S. Coast Guard Brat and U.S. Air Force Spouse

Expect that you are also going to change while your spouse is gone. You may become more independent, and that's a good thing. You're going to need to be to take care of everything that could happen.

There is no magic elixir to make the time you are away from someone you love go any faster or feel less lonely. There are only the seconds, minutes, hours, and days themselves.

> A big thing to remember when you are just starting military life together is there are other spouses around you that are experiencing the same or similar things that you are. I found it is important to make friends, and sometimes this may mean you have to reach out to them because they are afraid to reach out.
>
> —Rebecca Roth, U.S. Air Force Spouse

How you choose to fill the time apart, however, can make a big difference in your overall quality of life.

The following suggestions may give you some good ideas.

- Establish a family routine and stick to it as much as possible. A routine is like comfort food. It tastes good when you don't feel good.
- Participate in the unit's family readiness group where you will not only find the support and friendship of others sharing the same experience but also you may be privy to unit news sooner rather than later.
- Watch your words. Don't overshare any routine or logistical news you happen to learn about the unit while they're gone. Again, this is an important safety precaution. One benign statement could put someone you love (including yourself) directly in harm's way. In this world, you also hear about bad things when they do happen far away first, well before the national news cycle or the DoD has time to process the information. While your true intentions of posting the news may be good, remember to be respectful of the privacy

of others. No one wants to learn about his or her life-changing bad news through Facebook first.

- Improve your job marketability while your spouse is gone. Enroll in a certificate or degree program. It will make the time seem to go faster, and you will be learning something useful out of it in the process.
- Indulge in a favorite hobby or try out a new one.
- Set a significant fitness goal. Train for a 5K or commit to improved health.
- Reach out to the new spouse in the unit. He or she will be eternally grateful.
- If you subscribe to retail therapy, shop responsibility. You don't need debt or added debt.
- Cut your hair or let it grow. Think ombre. Or not.
- Volunteer in your community, doing something that makes you feel good inside.
- Volunteer in your community, doing something new that you can add to your skill set and future marketability.

> Grow some ba%%s and be okay with being alone for extended periods of time.
> You will need them as you will HAVE to do everything and then some by yourself most or some of the time.
>
> —Anonymous, OCONUS Military Spouse

- Email your sweetheart everyday, even if he doesn't have access. Skip sending him the racy photos if he may be living somewhere receiving your cheeky shots could land him in trouble.
- Make a point to leave your house routinely. Staying isolated won't be helpful.
- Reach out and ask for help if you feel like you need help. It shows you have true strength.
- Don't overcommit yourself. You're stressed out enough as it is.
- Plan and execute a girls' night out complete with fruity drinks. Arrange for reliable childcare (if necessary) and a designated driver (definitely necessary).
- Don't wait around for his phone call. It will come when it comes, and hopefully you will be around to answer it when it does.

- Read every book on the current bestseller list.
- Rent and watch every [you fill in the blank] movie ever made.
- Find a mantra that works for you and repeat it each morning.
- Plan a trip to someplace you've always wanted to go and go there.
- Get a new job or get yourself promoted in your old one.
- Keep your spouse present in the house, even though he isn't there logistically.
- Don't overdose and speculate on world news.
- Set a financial goal that everyone can enjoy on your spouse's return.
- Take the time to do something nice for yourself weekly.
- Focus on your kids if you have them. They need your attention now more than ever.
- Accept that some days won't be easy, and drive on.
- Help narrow the gap between the military and civilian worlds. Befriend a civilian. They don't bite.
- Journal your thoughts, feelings, fears, and joys.
- Create a countdown calendar.

Always hope for the best, but be prepared for the curveballs.

—Anonymous, OCONUS Military Spouse

- Don't expect him to sound carefree and happy when you do get to hear his voice.
- Meditate.
- Practice deep breathing.
- Sign up for a new class at the fitness center.
- If you are feeling very overwhelmed and sad, talk to a Military Family Life Consultant (MFLC). You can find out how to contact one at the military family support center.
- Get enough sleep.
- Exercise routinely.
- Eat healthy meals and stay hydrated.

When counting down the time until your spouse's return, my grandpa (a very wise, retired U.S. Air Force LtCol) always told me to "never count the week you're in or the week he gets back. It will make time go by quicker."

—Pam Cabana Macken, U.S. Air Force (Retired) and U.S. Air Force Brat

Helping Your Kids Survive and Thrive

If military life sometimes seems unfair to you, imagine how it must feel to those who were unwillingly born into it. Military brats (a term of affection) are a resilient lot, but even the toughest among them can have a hard time when one or even both parents are out of the picture on a day-to-day basis.

Keeping the universe in balance isn't always easy when your family is split up. Expect a range of feelings, sometimes on a daily basis. Just like you, your children are going to have good days and bad days. It's up to you, dear super parent, to keep them grounded and to help them get through this trying time.

No matter how hard you try, you won't be able to shield them from the sadness, pain, and loneliness that come along with not seeing Mom or Dad everyday. Tears are going to fall at times. At times, they will be your tears, too.

In the end here, all you can do is your best. Try to keep your family on track with some degree of structure and as much consistency as you can muster. This may be a challenging time for everyone, near and far, but it will eventually pass.

There are ample resources out there today that can help you help your kids though a deployment. As is the often the case, however, there are so many that drilling it down to what you need at the moment can be overwhelming.

Preparing Children for Deployment on the Department of Defense's Real Warriors website (http://www.realwarriors.net) does an excellent job of telling you what you need to know now.

The Real Warriors site "is a multimedia public awareness campaign designed to encourage help-seeking behavior among service members, veterans and military families coping with invisible wounds." There's lots of great information on it. Check it out.

Here are their reworded, condensed, and at times, embellished suggestions:

Before the love of your life deploys to parts unknown, have a frank and open discussion about the kids. Clearly identify any important points of contention, and discuss them while you have actual face time with one another. Also, plan your strategy for determining when and how you're going to tell your children about the upcoming deployment.

Think about the age of your kids before you open your mouth. A baby, for example, may not know that Mom is leaving, but you can bet he senses the increased stress levels around him. Your teenager, on the other hand, can understand better what is going on. Depending on the ages of your children, a different concept of time (as in when Mom is coming home) may apply.

Plan family meetings before the deployment. Family meetings allow everyone to get together and learn the facts together. Your kids should be included in any planning processes where possible so that they know they are a part of the bigger picture.

Establish and encourage open communication. This is something you should have with your children all the time, not just during stressful times when you need to have it the most.

Allow questions and answers. Encourage your kids to ask questions about the upcoming separation, and do your best to honestly and age appropriately answer them.

Talk about how the kids can keep connected to the deploying parent. Renegotiate responsibilities around the house if necessary.

Create connections that will last through the miles. Quality family time may have to be carved out of busy predeployment activities, but do it. Whatever it is that you usually do for fun, do it now. Be present in the moment and value the experience.

Also consider exchanging items that mean something with one another.

Real Warriors suggests, for example, that items for older children could include such items as a favorite pillow, T-shirt, or baseball cap, while younger children might appreciate a voice recording of the deploying parent reading a story or saying a few words.

The memories and touchstones created here may keep everyone emotionally connected to each other while your loved one is away.

Handling the Holidays Apart

It's hard to be apart from the one you love at any time, but it can be especially difficult during the holidays or on special occasions. It can be equally hard or even harder for your deployed spouse as well.

If you stay a military family for any length of time, it's bound to happen sooner or later, however. If and when it happens to you, it may help to draw on creative coping strategies while you do your best to be strong for everyone else you care about, near and far.

One way to mark the holidays is to continue established family traditions even though your spouse is not present. You might even consider creating a life-sized cutout figure of your spouse and including him in the festivities. Record the gathering and let everyone say a few special words for him and then send it to him.

Or not. You know your spouse better than anyone. If you think he will appreciate it, send it. If you think it will only bring him down, wait and share it with him when he returns.

You and your family members can also create an old-fashioned or virtual scrapbook of your holiday. Recruit everyone in the project, and create a wonderful keepsake of the season, including photos from your deployed spouse. Take pictures of family members on Skype with Mom or Dad downrange. Create a play-by-play of the season, and share it with your spouse on his or her return home.

Create a new family tradition that includes your deployed spouse somehow virtually. For example, depending on where your loved one is stationed, you might be able to facilitate an ornament swap.

Consider doing something nice for someone else with no strings attached. Include your children in the act, and reinforce the importance of charity outside the home. It will show them that even when you have your own issues to deal with, like deployment, you can think outside of yourself and relate to others in a generous way. Not surprisingly, you'll see a lot of this kind of behavior in our military communities during the holidays and throughout the year, too.

Don't try to do it all. You'll only become overwhelmed and frustrated. Pick and choose the must-do items on your holiday to-do list. If your spouse is the go-to guy for hanging up all the holiday lights on the trim of the house and you have no desire to climb a ladder, then don't. Instead, take the kids on local road trips to see lights elsewhere in your community. Next year he can do it.

Holidays and special occasions can be stressful times, so make a concerted effort to take care of yourself physically, mentally, spiritually, and emotionally, too.

DEMOBILIZATION: ANTICIPATION

This is a very military sounding word that simply means that the unit (and the love of your life) is coming back home. You couldn't be more excited. You may or may not know exact details early in this stage, but you can begin to design the Welcome Home posters now. Sooner or later, the plane, train, automobile, or ship will actually arrive back home. Let the partying begin.

POSTDEPLOYMENT/REINTEGRATION
AND REUNION

The day you've been waiting for will finally happen. If things fall into place the way they should, you will consider it to be the happiest day of your life. You will smile so much your face will actually hurt while hot tears of joy blur your vision. You will only hope that your touch tells him what your words fail to say.

You're home. You're safe. I love you.

If you're lucky, someone will record the moment and post it somewhere on the Internet. Your homecoming story will become a massively viral sensation resulting in enough generated advertising revenue to pay for your child's future college tuition. (One can dream, right?)

After the video stops recording, though, the hard work of living together after living apart for so long begins. Realize you both have been in different places, doing different and important things. For better or worse, you might be different people to a certain degree now.

You will be excited and anxiously waiting for that moment, but you might also be a bit apprehensive, too. You may wonder if your spouse has changed and how he has changed. You may wonder how he will respond to you, too.

The postdeployment period can last from a few weeks to several months. Don't be surprised if you get stressed out and frustrated along the way about how marital roles and responsibilities are renegotiated.

The reintegration process is a process indeed, and it will take time to go through. It helps to have strategies at the ready.

> TDYs [and other separations] are tough for everyone. Allow time for adjustment upon return. You've both lived on your own for a while and done things your way.
>
> Coming back together as a team is not always easy.
>
> —Pam Cabana Macken, U.S. Air Force (Retired) and U.S. Air Force Brat

- Plan to be patient with each other. Talk openly to one another and include your children in age-appropriate discussions.
- Cut your kids some slack as they adjust to having a full house once again.
- Considerately strive to become reacquainted with each other again. Don't revive old assumptions in the process.

- Start planning mandatory family fun, but don't force it too quickly.
- Don't expect too much from each other in the beginning.
- If you sense your spouse is feeling alone and having difficulty adjusting, encourage him to seek counseling.
- Try to maintain a positive and nonjudgmental attitude. There may be uncomfortable moments as you and your service member get reacquainted and begin rebuilding your relationship. The right attitude will help to lower stress and frustration when getting back together doesn't seem to be going the way you expected.
- Share your experiences during the deployment and how you've changed. It can help you reestablish a foundation of healthy communication and encourage your service member to trust you with his or her deployment experiences.
- Try to be patient. It may be some time before you and your spouse feel relaxed and comfortable together. You may have to modify your expectations often during the postdeployment period, so it's important to keep in mind that time and patience are critical to the process of recovering from combat experience.
- Start making new dreams together. It will help you feel closer as you begin to move forward together, finally, again.

Theoretically, everyone experiences one cycle of deployment and then gets a break. One certainly deserves a break at that point, anyway. Reality, however, doesn't always happen that way. It's not unheard of for phases four and one to collide in a spectacularly stressful kind of way.

Know how to do the whole routine (bills, cooking, lawn mowing) on your own.

—Siggi, U.S. Air Force Spouse

7

DIFFICULT TOPICS IN MILITARY LIFE

Military family life is full of unique experiences, wonderful people, and interesting opportunities.

Except when it's not.

Bad things happen in military life, just as they do in life outside the main gate of every installation in the world. People don't like to talk about those bad things, but they are real. Denying their existence won't make them disappear.

Some of those bad experiences are relatively minor in nature. Some are even of the self-imposed variety. You get a parking ticket or you forget to pay a bill. A check bounces (once). These are embarrassing mistakes, but they aren't necessarily career enders or life changers unless you repeatedly fail to learn from them.

Other bad experiences could have far-reaching implications.

They could happen as a result of any number of stressors commonplace to military life. They could happen because of ignorance or the inability to control emotions, or they could happen simply because they are destined to do so.

Difficult topics such as bullying, depression, suicide, sexual assault, domestic violence, combat injuries, and death are what we will discuss in this chapter specifically.

Why Be Such a Downer Now?

Why bring up this kind of negativity in a book designed to orient you to the basics about military life in an encouraging way?

In or out of the military community, negativity exists. Your aware-ness of it and what to do when you see or experience it yourself could be lifesaving.

Welcome not just to Military Life 101 but to Life 101.

> A big thing that is hard for a lot of type-A spouses is you do not have control of what is happening around you with the military. There are times your spouse has to work late, do a weeklong field training exercise, go on TDY (travel to another place to work for short periods of time), or you get orders to move to someplace you have never heard of. You learn quickly that you have no control.
>
> —Rebecca Roth, U.S. Air Force Spouse

You may never be the victim of domestic violence or sexual assault, but somewhere along the way, you might meet a fellow military spouse who is who needs your help whether she knows to ask for it or not.

You may never get the knock on your door that breaks your heart and forever changes your life, but the person living next door to you might. If you are the first one on the scene, will you know how to render comfort and guidance?

Your own spouse may deploy to a war zone one day and come back as someone you don't even recognize, physically, mentally, or emotionally. What happens then?

Are you starting to understand the reason for this particular chapter in your basic training?

You may or may not be touched by the negativity that any life has to offer, but you should at least be able to recognize it when you see it and know where to go for more help when it's needed.

> If you find that you need or want assistance, services are available all over the military. It is smart and resourceful to seek out these services and utilize them. Family Advocacy and Family Support offer classes and support groups on re-lationships, parenting, and managing emotions. Installation Mental/Behavioral Health Clinics offer counseling services. Additionally, there are many indepen-dent mental health care practitioners on the economy that accept insurance or who can be paid privately. Some providers even offer distance counseling, so no matter where we are in the world, we still have resources!
>
> —Jennifer Oswalt, U.S. Air Force Spouse

THE RISE OF ONLINE HATERS

Someone takes a photo of someone else without their knowledge or consent or perhaps copies it off of someone's Facebook page and posts it online elsewhere along with nasty remarks about their physical appearance or what they might be doing.

No, it's not grade school, although it sounds a lot like it.

It's cyberbullying, and it's nothing new, just ask any teenager.

The rise of adult military community members verbally attacking fellow adult military community members within social media, however, is relatively new and highly disappointing.

It is also quite unexpected in a world that has traditionally been supportive of its own by virtue of common ground and those perhaps incorrectly assumed concepts of honor and maturity.

Exactly why this has occurred is unclear. Some people clearly have unresolved issues in their lives.

There is much speculation that an entitlement mentality among some military spouses and the reciprocal backlash against it by others could be to blame for online haters. We could also point to narcissism, impulsiveness, and just plain meanness in people, too. Perhaps it is even a symptom of a much bigger and darker issue throughout the services with regard to how women are treated both in and out of uniform. Oh, that it weren't so, right?

If You or Someone You Know Is Targeted

Let's be clear. There is no reason for anyone to negatively stereotype anyone else in the military community where its members, in uniform or not, are theoretically held to a higher unwritten standard of behavior.

For one military spouse to treat another military spouse like this is taking sad to a shameful new level.

That said, you know that someone eventually will do it again because stupidity can be quite resilient. Even though we like to think that those in the military family are above this kind of behavior, some people are simply not.

So, if you or someone you know is the center of attention in this negative way, avoid responding to the harasser, as he or she would like nothing more than to make you upset and have you engage at that low level.

Instead, capture screenshots as proof and report the incident immediately as admins might be able to disable the offensive exchange.

If you feel physically threatened in any way, report the incident to law enforcement. If you suspect an online attack is being made by a fellow member of the military community, contact the military police, too.

Check and recheck your privacy settings online. Adjust them as necessary.

Perhaps even more importantly, think preventatively before you post. Once you put it out there online, there is no retrieving it. Ever.

> Ensure that you are taking care of yourself. Providing your body with good nutrition and adequate sleep and exercise is especially important during times of stress.
>
> —Jennifer Oswalt, U.S. Air Force Spouse

STRESSED OUT: EMOTION COMMOTION

Everyone feels stressed at one time or another. It can be a healthy thing, spurring you on to greatness through adversity. Too much stress, however, can backfire on you physically, emotionally, and mentally.

> Set aside time for you. If you have kiddos, this will be especially important. Seek out affordable childcare options, perhaps a high-schooler or home day-care provider, to ensure that you have time to do what makes you happy.
>
> —Jennifer Oswalt, U.S. Air Force Spouse

How do you know if you're feeling a tad too stressed out and letting your emotions run amok, amok, amok?

You may:

- feel moody or irritable
- let the smallest things set you off
- be agitated and/or find yourself unable to relax
- feel very overwhelmed
- feel lonely and isolated from others
- be depressed or unhappy
- experience aches and pains
- be constipated or have diarrhea

- have chest pains or experience frequent colds
- find that you don't like doing things you used to do

Not only does stress do a number on you emotionally and physically but also it can mess with you mentally. It can make you:

- forget things easily
- have difficulty concentrating
- lack good judgment when it comes to decision making
- be negative and worry about everything

What happens when all of that stress becomes too much to handle? We go to the extreme of things, of course.

We may eat too much or too little, causing unhealthy fluctuations in our weight. We may not get enough sleep, or we may sleep all the time. We may become a drinking, smoking, drug-taking, nail-biting, floor-pacing hot mess of an individual.

How very charming, no?

> Minimize trips to the food court as much as possible and seek out healthy food options. Most installations have a gym/wellness center. Take advantage of the classes and programs available.
>
> —Jennifer Oswalt, U.S. Air Force Spouse

> Stay physically fit! A good run, walk, or lifting session can burn tons of stress!! A family who lifts together stays together.
>
> —Denise Wright, Military Spouse

How to Calm Yourself

If you're at a point where something has to change, then go all Gandhi on yourself and be the change you want to see in the world.

- Take slow, deep, purposeful breaths. Let your lungs enjoy a taste of real oxygen. Give your stressed-out, overworked heart an opportunity to slow way down.

- Learn how to meditate and practice daily. Learn how to effectively focus your breathing and thoughts as they drift through your mind.
- Focus on the things you can control. If you can't control it, think like Disney's Elsa on *Frozen* and just let it go.
- Learn how to say no and mean it. You don't have to agree to do everything anyone asks. Saying *no* can be liberating.
- Take care of yourself physically, too. Eat right and exercise regularly. Get enough sleep. Invest in a Fitbit or similar product and begin to gain a real awareness of your activity level. Challenge yourself to a higher level of health. If you are having a difficult time doing this, take advantage of the dietitian and wellness center professionals on the installation. You can find them through the military treatment facility (aka health care clinic).

Know when to ask for help. Showing your imperfection and asking for help helps others let their guards down and do the same.

—Siggi, U.S. Air Force Spouse

THE WARNING SIGNS OF DEPRESSION AND SUICIDE

Dark times can creep into the lives of everyone, including service members, military spouses, teenagers, and even younger children. No one in the military family is immune.

The emotional signs of depression are varied and many. They could include feelings of sadness, anger, frustration, or irritability. Someone who is depressed could lose interest in normal activities. He may experience feelings of worthlessness, self-blame, or self-criticism and exhibit a need for excessive reassurance. People who are depressed are unable to concentrate, make decisions, or remember details.

These types of feelings go far beyond the precoffee feelings of a Monday morning. Those who are depressed may even have thoughts of death, dying, or suicide.

There are other signs that someone may be experiencing a rough time, too, signs that can be observed in the way he or she behaves.

The behavioral signs of depression could include:

- tiredness or loss of energy
- changes in sleeping patterns
- changes in appetite
- abuse of alcohol or drugs
- restlessness; an inability to sit still
- complaints of not feeling well all the time
- neglected physical appearance
- disruptive or risky behavior
- self-harm (such as cutting, burning, eraser burning, excessive tattooing, or body piercing)

What can you do when you suspect someone you know may be depressed?

Keep the lines of communication open. Don't be judgmental. Practice active listening, maintaining eye contact and nodding your head to acknowledge you hear what is being said. Be a friend, or at the very least, be present enough in the moment to realize what may be going on right before your eyes.

Encourage that person to reach out for professional assistance.

It's important for someone struggling to get the help he needs because depression can lead to suicide, too, which is a big concern for our community.

The suicide rate among veterans, for example, has doubled since 2005.[1] Just exactly why that is, no one is certain, although many theories abound.

It's important that we know how to recognize the warning signs when they appear and we know what to do about it.

Some of the warning signs of suicide include:

- a low mood that doesn't seem to go away
- pessimism
- hopelessness
- desperation
- anxiety, psychic pain, and inner tension
- withdrawal
- sleep problems

Individuals thinking about suicide might also show an increased use of alcohol and/or other drugs. Individuals may seem to act more impulsively or begin taking unnecessary risks.

The person who is contemplating suicide may even tell us that they are thinking it. They may verbally threaten to kill themselves or express a death wish. The statement *just shoot me now*, used in jest by some, may be more than a joke here.

Someone who is seriously playing with the idea of killing himself may begin to give away the things that once mattered a great deal to him. He may begin to logically plan how to off himself, too, by gathering the necessary weapon, poison, or medication.

Unexpected rage or anger is not uncommon, either.

Some of the warnings signs can even seem commonplace when you think about them individually. When you string a few of those signs together, it may not even mean someone is thinking about suicide then, but don't discount the possibility, either.

> Military OneSource is an excellent source of information.
>
> —Jennifer Oswalt, U.S. Air Force Spouse

What You Can Do

Mental Health America offers these tips if you suspect someone is thinking about suicide:

- If you think someone is in danger, trust your instincts.
- Communicate your concerns to that person and listen, really listen, to what is said.
- Ask specific questions in order to see if a plan has been devised.
- Get professional help even if the person objects. Don't try to be the expert.
- Don't leave the person alone, and do not promise to keep the conversation secret.
- Don't make personal judgments in the situation.

Lifeline Resources

Service members and families who need support are encouraged to call the Military Crisis Line at 800-273-TALK (800-273-8255). It offers free and confidential support for those in crisis.

You can also learn more about these topics at:

- Defense Suicide Prevention Office, www.suicideoutreach.org
- Veterans Crisis Line Online Chat, http://www.veteranscrisisline.net
- Military Crisis Line, 800-273-8255
- Military OneSource, http://www.militaryonesource.mil/
- your military installation's chaplain
- your military installation's medical treatment facility

> Don't try to appear perfect. Let people see your strengths and weaknesses. Use your strengths to help other military spouses and families when you can, even if they don't ask for it but you see the need.
>
> —Siggi, U.S. Air Force Spouse

SEXUAL ASSAULT AND DOMESTIC ABUSE

There is a current slogan in the Army that says: Sexual Assault: Not in Our Army. But it is. It is in our Army even if recent statistics show a decrease in cases reported.[2] It also exists in other branches of the service. Domestic abuse exists, too.

Whether the victims or perpetrators wear a uniform or not, both crimes happen every day, and sadly, many go unreported. Spouses, in particular, may be hesitant to report sexual assault or abuse because they don't want to negatively impact their spouse's career.

According to the National Domestic Violence Hotline (NDVH), domestic violence can be defined as a pattern of behavior in any relationship that is used to gain or maintain power over an intimate partner.

- It happens to those who wear the uniform and to those who don't.
- It doesn't matter how much money you earn or what rank your service member spouse holds.
- Your educational level, your profession, the color of your skin, and the religion you choose to practice or not is irrelevant.
- Your age and where you were born and raised don't matter, either.

Domestic violence is an equal opportunity crime. Anyone can be a victim, but women are more likely to be victims than men.

According to the Centers for Disease Control and Prevention (CDC), one in four women and one in nine men in the United States are victims of domestic violence at some point in their lives. Six in ten U.S. adults claim they know someone personally who has experienced it.

Those numbers are more than likely inaccurate as many incidences of domestic violence are underreported.

Someone may be a victim of domestic abuse if:

- She is usually an open and outgoing person but she becomes suddenly quiet or withdrawn around her spouse.
- She has an unexplained injury like a black eye or a swollen lip and she tries to cover it up somehow with clothing or makeup.
- She isolates herself from others altogether.

It's a given that the basic hardships of military life for some could also be contributing factors. Frequent relocations, multiple deployments, reintegration challenges, and dealing with new realities as a result of combat-related disabilities, PTSD, and TBI could easily add to anyone's stress level.

According to NDVH, you may be in an emotionally abusive relationship if your partner:

- calls you names, insults you, or constantly criticizes you
- shows a lack of trust
- exhibits jealously or possessiveness
- attempts to isolate you from friends or family
- constantly monitors your activities
- doesn't want you to go to work
- controls all the finances and/or refuses to share money with you
- withholds affection as punishment
- expects you to always ask permission to do things
- threatens to hurt you, other family members, or pets

You may be in a physically abusive relationship if your partner has ever:

- damaged property when angry
- pushed, slapped, bitten, kicked, or choked you
- left you alone in a dangerous or unfamiliar place
- scared you by reckless driving
- threatened or hurt you with a weapon
- prevented you from leaving or trapped you at home

- hurt your children
- used physical force in sexual situations

You may be in a sexually abusive relationship if your partner:

- views women as objects and believes in rigid gender roles
- accuses you of having an affair
- is jealous of your other outside relationships
- insults you in sexual ways or calls you sexual names
- has ever forced sex or held you down during it
- demanded sex when you were sick, tired, or after beating you
- used weapons or objects to hurt you during sex
- involved others in sexual activities
- ignored your feelings regarding sex

What to Do About It

Confront someone you suspect of being abused and tell her about your suspicions. Let her know about the possible resources available to her.

In the military community, victims don't always understand that confidential help is available thorough the Victim Advocacy Program (VAP).

The VAP provides services to victims of domestic violence and sexual assault such as crisis intervention, safety planning, medical assistance, information on how to obtain legal assistance, and referral to shelters. It is a voluntary program that works closely with the Family Advocacy Program (FAP) on military installations worldwide.

For example, with restricted reporting, no investigations are initiated unless it is determined that a life is endangered. With unrestricted reporting, however, the service member's command is notified and an investigation is launched.

If a victim calls the police (military or civilian) first instead of a victim advocate, then it is automatically considered unrestricted reporting, and there may be an investigation.

Abusers are also able to get help through individual counseling, domestic violence support groups, and/or anger management classes. They may also be ordered to have a psychological evaluation. The abuser could also be responsible for treatment costs if mandated to treatment through a civilian court system.

Help ensure that your home is a safe place for open communication. Be sure to know and take advantage of your resources. Develop a support network. Seek help when you need it. Trust that difficult times won't last and that the bumps in the road will smooth out.

—Jennifer Oswalt, U.S. Air Force Spouse

Signs of Abuse and Neglect in a Child

Domestic violence doesn't just happen to grown-ups. It can happen to innocent children, too. A child who is being abused may:

- show a sudden change in behavior or school performance
- perform poorly on a regular basis in school
- have unattended medical or physical needs even after the caregivers are notified
- have a hard time concentrating
- have poor language development and perceptual and motor skills
- appear to be anxious
- appear to lack adult supervision
- be overly compliant, passive, or withdrawn
- seem to be afraid of his home and may try to avoid going there
- may be self-destructive
- express a dislike of his parent(s) or guardian(s)
- have unexplained physical injuries

Here are the potential signs of a parent or guardian who may be being abusive to a child:

- He shows little or no concern for the child.
- He denies the existence of the child's problems in school or at home.
- He blames the child for problems in his or her life.
- He gives other authority figures the green light to use harsh, physical discipline if the child misbehaves.
- He sees the child as entirely bad, worthless, or burdensome.
- He expects too much of the child, demanding a level of physical or academic performance the child cannot achieve.
- He expects his child to fulfill his own emotional needs.

- He doesn't often touch or even look at the child.
- He doesn't like being a parent or a guardian.
- He tells others that he doesn't like his child.
- He seems depressed or behaves irrationally.
- He abuses drugs and/or alcohol.
- He has a history of being abused as a child himself.

What You Can Do

There are plenty of things you can do to help yourself or someone you know in cases of sexual assault, domestic abuse, and child abuse. The resources are many.

The DoD Safe Helpline[3] Victims may call the DoD Safe Helpline at 001-877-995-5247. The DoD Safe Helpline is a crisis support service specially designed to provide live, one-on-one support to sexual assault survivors and their loved ones within the DoD community.

All helpline services are confidential, anonymous, secure, and available worldwide, providing survivors with the help they need, anytime, anywhere.

Safe Helpline staff members have been trained to answer questions relating to military specific topics such as Restricted and Unrestricted Reporting and how to connect with relevant military resources, such as an installation or base's Sexual Assault Response Coordinator (SARC), should those services be requested.

You can also access the Safe Helpline online at www.safehelpline.org, where you have access to live, confidential, one-on-one help through a secure instant-messaging platform. The website also contains information about recovering from and reporting a sexual assault.

On the website there is also a Safe HelpRoom (www.safehelproom .org), where survivors can chat with and support each other online. The HelpRoom is safe, moderated, and open 24/7.

The DoD Safe Helpline app allows survivors to create a customized self-care plan and access recommended exercises. Self-care plans and exercises can be accessed anytime, even without an Internet connection. You can also use the app to call Safe Helpline for free no matter where you're stationed, and the app is available on any iOS or Android device for free.

Finally, you can text the DoD Safe Helpline by sending your zip code or installation and base name to 55-247 (in the United States) or 202-470-5546 (outside the United States). Someone will quickly text you back with contact information for the nearest civilian or DoD sexual assault service provider. Text message and data rates may apply.

You can also contact the military police, a local law enforcement agency, or the family advocacy program at the family service support center on your military installation.

Other Helpful Related Resources

- National Child Abuse Hotline, (800) 422-4453
- DoD Child Abuse Hotline, (800) 336-4592
- About Child Abuse and Neglect, www.childwelfare.gov
- Safe Horizons, www.safehorizons.org
- Victim Assistance, www.ncvc.org

Recognizing a Child Predator

It's hard to find the words to even write about the monsters that sickeningly prey on innocent children. It's equally difficult to hear about them living in and around our military communities, but they do. Just Google anyplace for the list of registered sex offenders database if you doubt it.

Child predators target and groom potential victims by:

- making friends with parents to get closer to their kids
- working around children in either paid or volunteer capacities
- hanging out in places where kids are likely to be
- interacting with them online, often pretending to be someone they are not
- becoming foster parents, giving them in-house access to potential victims or a reason to be around other children

What Can You Do?

- Don't pretend predators don't exist. Learn about them so you can better identify one if the situation arises.
- Make sure your children understand, in an age-appropriate way, that there are bad grown-ups out there that may not have their best interest at heart.
- Know where your children are all the time. Know where they like to hang out and know who they like to hang out with.

- Teach your kids to safeguard personal information, on and offline, such as their name, address, telephone number, age, and email address.
- Troubleshoot bad situations with your children. Teach them the right answers to those "what would you do if . . ." scenarios.
- Develop a safety word with your child that he can use at any time with you to let you know things are not right.

If you suspect that your child or any child is being targeted and/or groomed by a child predator, get the facts together and go to the military police, the civilian law enforcement authorities, or child protective services.

DIVORCE IN THE MILITARY

You're young, in love, and perhaps you haven't been married very long, either. Even so, you probably know that every marriage has its share of ups and downs.

When the downs become truly insurmountable, then divorce may become a reality. Here's hoping you never have to draw upon this knowledge, but just in case you need to know a couple of things, here you go.

The military views divorce as a private civil matter that should be addressed by a civilian court. The authority of military commanders in such situations is often limited.

Both spouses may request assistance through the military legal assistance office. Of course, if you're divorcing you'll each want a separate lawyer. Military lawyers may not be able to draft specific court documents or represent you in a civilian court, but they can still give you advice on legal issues regarding divorce and child custody, income taxes, the Servicemembers Civil Relief Act, and wills.

Spouses of service members may not be entitled to continued military benefits after a divorce unless two specific circumstances are met.

The 20/20/20 Rule

If you and your spouse should decide to get a divorce, you will not continue to receive military benefits unless you have been married to him a very long time.

An unmarried former spouse may receive medical, commissary, exchange, and theater privileges if he or she meets something called the

20/20/20 rule. That means the spouse was married to the service member for at least twenty years at the time of the divorce, dissolution, or annulment.

The military member must have served for at least twenty years of creditable service in determining eligibility for retired pay *and* the former spouse was married to the service member during at least twenty years of that period of creditable service.

The 20/20/15 Rule

If you don't meet the strict requirements of the 20/20/20 rule, you might be able to obtain one year of transitional medical military benefits only if you meet the 20/20/15 rule. There's still quite a bit time involved here, too.

In this instance, the service member would have to have served at least twenty years of creditable service and the marriage must have lasted for twenty years, too. The period of marriage must have overlapped the period of service by at least fifteen years.

There are also laws in place that you and your soon-to-be-ex service member in this case should know about, such as the Uniformed Services Former Spouse Protection Act. This is a federal law that provides certain benefits such as retirement pay, medical care, and use of exchanges and commissaries to former spouses of military members.

The Servicemembers Civil Relief Act provides a wide range of protections for those who serve in uniform. It is intended to postpone or suspend certain civil obligations in the name of duty. In the case of divorce, it may allow a service member to obtain a "stay" or postponement of court proceedings because of duty requirements.

Before you and your spouse resort to dissolving your marriage, consider going to marital counseling first.

Military and Family Life Counselors (MFLCs) can provide help with a number of topics to include relationship issues, conflict resolution, anger management, and communication skills.

CARING FOR A WOUNDED WARRIOR

Life isn't always fair to those we love. Sometimes they can get hurt in combat, suffer a serious illness, or become injured as a result of an accident.

While there are ample resources and support available to assist us, it is still up to us to take care of them twenty-four hours a day, seven days a week, for however long it takes, and that can be hard.

If your spouse is gravely injured or ill, expect there to be a long road of recovery, rehabilitation, and ultimately reintegration.

To cope with the situation, get smart about it. Learn all you can about the injury or illness and encourage your spouse to do the same.

Create a plan of attack. Figure out what needs to happen next. Your spouse may need to go through a military medical evaluation process, also called a *med board*. Depending on the results of the med board, he may return to duty, or he could be required to transition out of service. It doesn't hurt to think about the future possibilities and begin planning for those contingencies.

If your spouse does indeed have to separate from service due to an injury or illness, there may be VA benefits available for your service member as a result. Make sure you are well versed in his potential postuniform benefits and entitlements. The military transition center can help you. Read chapter 8, "Mission Transition," too.

Caregiver Coping Skills

- Accepting that life is different is a hard reality to handle. Take a deep, deep breath and handle it anyway.
- Continue to live your life.
- Be honest with family members and close friends.
- Embrace the new reality and move forward together positively.

Each branch of service operates a wounded warrior program designed to assist service members and their families with nonmedical issues that are associated with returning to duty or transitioning back into the civilian world.

Enrollment information about each of the programs can be found here:

- Army Wounded Warrior Program (AW2), http://www.wtc.army .mil
- Marine Corps Wounded Warrior Regiment (WWR), http://www .woundedwarriorregiment.org
- Navy Safe Harbor (NSH), http://safeharbor.navylive.dodlive.mil

- Air Force Wounded Warrior (AFW2), http://www.woundedwarrior
.af.mil/

The above organizations can help families that need it with a host of military-related issues, to include:

- pay and personnel issues
- invitational travel orders
- lodging and housing adaptations
- childcare arrangements
- legal issues
- education and training benefits
- respite care

Post-Traumatic Stress

Anyone who lives through a traumatic event can get post-traumatic stress. Suffering from it over the long haul can result in post-traumatic stress disorder (PTSD).

It should come as no surprise that military service members have found and will continue to find themselves in highly stressful situations. It's the nature of the job.

You should know a few things about it just in case your spouse or others around you experience it.

The symptoms of PTSD may occur right after the event that causes it, or it could be weeks, months, or even years before they appear. They can vary from person to person. While only a trained medical professional can diagnose PTSD, possible symptoms could include:

- flashbacks to the traumatic event, where the person experiencing it feels as if he was reliving that moment of time
- not talking about their traumatic experience or other things that may remind them of it. They don't like to be in situations that bring back those uneasy feelings, either.
- being stressed out to the point they are hyperaroused. They may have a hard time sleeping and be unable to concentrate, and they may be grumpy and feel like they are living a life on the edge.

PTSD not only affects the life of the person experiencing it but it can also affect family members and friends. Left unattended, it could change relationships, and not in a good way.

How You Can Help

If you suspect someone you know may be experiencing PTS or have PTSD, then encourage him or her to seek professional assistance. PTSD is treatable, but not unless those who can treat it know about it in the first place.

The military treatment facility (health clinic) or your own personal physician can be a good place to start.

If there is a crisis situation in progress, the National Center for PTSD[4] suggests you:

- call 911
- go to the nearest emergency room
- call the Suicide Prevention Lifeline at 1-800-273-8255
- contact the Veterans Crisis Line at 1-800-273-8255 (press 1) or initiate a Veterans Chat at www.veteranscrisisline.net.

Remember that you are a resilient military family—you've got this!

—Jennifer Oswalt, U.S. Air Force Spouse

CASUALTY ASSISTANCE AND SURVIVING LOSS

No one ever likes to imagine it, but the worst thing that can happen, does happen. It happens in life outside the military, and it certainly happens inside it.

Almost ironically, death is an inescapable part of life.

The Casualty Assistance Program

When a service member dies, regardless of the reason, the military assigns a casualty assistance officer or representative to help the next of kin with anything they need help with in that difficult time. For example, the casualty assistance office may provide transportation for family members of the deceased or assist them in applying for various benefits and entitlements. He may help them gather required paperwork and assist in funeral arrangements. He may help the family relocate to another place. Whatever the needs of the next of kin, the casualty assistance officer can provide that help.

Speaking of Death . . . Are Your Affairs in Order?

Those we love are often left behind to close out the business of what was once our life. That heartbreaking task will be easier for someone you love if you have given the matter thought in advance.

Your Last Will. Your service member has to have a last will. Do you have one, though? If you don't, it's time to get one. It doesn't cost you anything but your time and a trip to the legal office on the installation. If you don't have one when you die, the courts will make all those final decisions for you whether they were what you would have wanted or not.

You can think of your last will as a GPS you leave for the living after you're gone. It guides whomever you have left in charge of your final affairs. It tells him how to divide your assets and close out any outstanding bills or accounts in your name. It tells him to post that final sunset picture on your Instagram or otherwise let your online friends know that you won't be posting any more snarky comments.

In addition to a will, consider getting a living trust, which is a document used to transfer property to beneficiaries, usually by avoiding probate court. This will potentially save time and preserve the value of your assets for whomever you leave them to in the end.

A living will may be a good idea, too. It allows you to outline your health care wishes in advance. For example, if you should ever wind up on life support and not want to stay there for the remainder of your days, a living will gives your designated person the power to pull the plug on you.

A Letter of Instruction

To keep your family members from arguing over who gets your Pandora collection when you're gone, consider writing a letter of instruction or intent, too. It could save loved ones a lot of stress in the end.

It tells others where to find your last will, financial documents, and other important paperwork. Important paperwork that you may want to mention in such a letter includes insurance polices, birth certificates, DD 214 (this is the form a service member receives upon separation from service), VA disability information, pension information, 401(k) accounts, and your Social Security number as well as titles and deeds to any property you own or loans you owe on.

Consider including this kind of information in a letter of intent or instruction as well:

- all your account names, numbers, passwords, and PINS so a hacker doesn't have to be paid later to figure them out
- what your assets are, where they are located, and points of contact for them
- how you want to be interred for eternity and what kind of funeral you want to have
- where to find the key to your safe deposit box or the combo to the house safe
- your input for your future obituary
- your personal feelings about anything or the dark secrets you kept from everyone while you were alive
- a list of those people you want to be notified of your death
- instructions for the care of anything important to you left behind

A Power of Attorney. You may be used to getting a power of attorney from your active duty spouse to take care of business while he's off doing what the military tells him to do. You might want to return the favor and have one lying in wait for him at some point.

While wills and letters of instructions tells those left behind what do to with your stuff, a power of attorney or an advance directive says who can legally make it all happen for you.

If you have the sudden urge to create a will, write a letter of intent and/or obtain a power of attorney, visit the military legal office or the Staff Judge Advocate (JAG).

Surviving Loss

The business end of death is one thing. The grieving process, however, is quite another. The death of a loved one can affect everything in our life from the way we act to the way we physically feel to the way we think. There is no set time when grieving ends, either.

Grief can show up in a number of different symptoms, such as:

- anger
- breathlessness
- crying jags
- diarrhea
- difficulty concentrating
- difficulty sleeping

- disorganization
- feeling of being in a surreal place
- headaches
- headaches and dizziness
- hyperventilating
- increased heart rate
- irritability
- lack of appetite
- nausea
- restlessness
- sadness or depression
- seeing images of the dead person
- self-blaming
- tightness in your chest
- tiredness
- weight loss

Surviving loss, it would seem, is no easy matter for the living.

How You Can Help

If you find yourself around another military spouse who has lost her spouse, or anyone who has experienced a close death for that matter, don't try to fix that person's grief. While it may be hard to watch someone suffer through this sad process, it is one that must be experienced in order to begin healing.

What can you do then?

Acknowledge the loss, choosing your words thoughtfully. The military might have lost Sergeant Jones, but the spouse sitting in front of you lost the love of her life and the father of her children. "I'm sorry for the loss of your husband, David" will sound more sincere than "I'm sorry for the loss of Sergeant Jones."

Don't make assumptions about someone's beliefs, either, as you offer up any words of comfort.

Try to be genuinely helpful, tapping into whatever are your own strengths to best help that new widow and his or her family.

After you offer your heartfelt condolences, don't continue to focus on death. Instead of talking about how the deceased died, talk about how he lived.

After the funeral, don't disappear. Help the new widow out with the day-to-day business of regular life because it will be a long time before she may be able to truly manage alone.

Encourage those who have lost someone to:

- talk about their feelings with others
- avoid keeping the tears, anger, and numbness pent up inside
- avoid feeling overwhelmed by keeping up with the day-to-day business of life
- get enough sleep, eat a well-balanced diet, and exercise regularly
- avoid excessive use of alcohol
- get back into a regular, familiar routine as soon as possible
- avoid making major decisions until they're ready to do so with a clear mind
- reach out for help if they need it

If you want or need more information about this, here are some great resources:

- Gold Star Wives, http://www.goldstarwives.org
- Grief Net, http://www.griefnet.org
- No Greater Love, http://www.ngl.org
- Society of Military Widows, http://www.militarywidows.org
- Tragedy Assistance Program for Survivors, http://www.taps.org

8

MISSION TRANSITION

If I had to prioritize the list of things I will miss, I would definitely put the culture of being an active duty spouse at the very top. The sisterhood and sense of family "away from family" has no comparison. Supporting fellow spouses and family members along with the honor of supporting the soldier that I have loved for the last two decades is one of the toughest roles to move beyond. The list is endless for things I will miss about living this lifestyle. I have been afforded immense opportunities that make everyday suburbia seem undeniably mundane to me.

—Sonia Greer, U.S. Army Spouse

As hard as that may seem, the active duty military lifestyle won't always be your own. There will come a day when whoever serves in uniform in your family will no longer do so.

You might think you know when that will time will come, but the truth is that you don't know. No one does. Plans can change in a heartbeat for any number of reasons far beyond your control.

- The DoD may decide to cut costs and people again.
- You and your spouse may decide that your family is simply not cut out for a life of constant unpredictability so characteristic of this world.
- You or your spouse may get a better job offer elsewhere.
- You may accomplish your goals and want to move on to the next state of your life. *Have college degree. Will travel.*

- Your spouse's career field may become nonexistent or overpopulated.
- Real misfortune could strike, and your spouse could become physically, mentally, or otherwise incapable of doing his job in the military anymore.

Anything could happen at any time to change your plans.

That's why it's important to think about the end of your time in the military lifestyle now, in the very beginning of it.

MAKING NOW COUNT FOR LATER

If you want to be ready for the day you become a "civilian" family again, start now to think about how you would like life to look like then.

Give the following questions some serious thought. Have your spouse do the same, and when you're ready, compare your answers with each other.

- Where do you see you and your family living after your spouse transitions out of the service?
- What do you imagine you both will be doing professionally?
- Collectively, will you be making the kind of salary you need to make in order to have the quality of life you want?

Lucky for you, you don't need to have the answers to these questions right now. If you give them due thought now, however, answering them for real later will be easier because you did something positive about them in plenty of time.

For example, let's say you want to live in the great state of Colorado post military life. If you know that now, your service member may be able to arrange his career so that his last duty station is in that state.

If that actually happens (and it does all the time), then you will be a good position on many levels to make that final transition. It will not be completely pain-free, but it will be easier logistically and perhaps emotionally on everyone in your family.

We can also apply that same logic to your post-military-life careers.

For example's sake, let's assume your uniformed spouse works as a medic in a military treatment facility. When he ultimately transitions out of service, he wants to continue working in the health care industry doing the same job.

He knows he can do the job. You know he can. But can he legally do that job postuniform on the basis of his military experience, or not?

Many who serve in uniform transition out of the military with documented training and experience that isn't necessarily recognized by state licensing entities. And some jobs require employees to have specific state licensure in order to legally work in that job.

If your spouse waits until the end of his career to discover that little reality, he will be disappointed.

On the other hand, if he thinks about that now and obtains the license he needs before he transitions out, he will be more marketable when the time comes.

In other words, while you are both living la vida military, you should both forward think about the transferability of any professional certifications while you have time to address it.

Both you and your uniformed spouse should plan to take full advantage of any educational assistance available to you. To find out more about available tuition assistance, visit the education center on the military installation. (See chapter 5, "Military Spouse Careers and Education," for more information.)

Where you ultimately live and what you do professionally in life after being a military family are big topics, but they aren't the only ones to think about.

Think about your postuniform financial future, too.

Right now, you may be a relatively new family or at least new to the military. It might just be the two of you, or you could have children.

Either way, fast-forward in your mind a few years. There is a real possibility that your needs and your family's will change and grow.

We all go through different ages and stages of life in which our wants, needs, and priorities shift.

The Short View versus the Long View

Setting and achieving concrete, short-term financial goals is easy. You know how to do that, right? Just for example's sake, let's say you want to go on a vacation next summer. You're thinking something exotic in an island kind of way. Islands are good. You pull out your calculator and estimate the costs.

You're going to have to get to that island somehow, and when you do, you'll want to eat, drink, sleep, and be greatly entertained. You make an educated guess about how much all that will cost you, and then you divide that number by the number of paydays you have left until you pack your bags.

If you haven't decided that you need to play the lottery and hope for the best, you will smartly save a certain portion from incoming paychecks until you can sip margaritas under a palm tree.

Short term is easy. Financially planning for life after the military, however, seems more abstract, doesn't it? It's so far away (*you think*), and there are so many other things to focus on now instead.

Let's stop and think for a minute about what you *don't* want to happen financially along the way.

- You don't want to miss out on saving a portion of your salaries for ultimate retirement. You're young now and supposedly have the luxury of time and compound interest on your side.
- You don't want to wake up one morning and realize you have a child going off to college who thinks you're going to pay the tuition bills and you haven't saved enough to make that a possibility.
- You don't want to live paycheck to paycheck forever.
- You don't want to be so far in debt that employers won't hire you because of it.
- You don't want to be financially illiterate, allowing others to take advantage of you and preventing you from ever getting ahead.

If you take the time to think about and *do something* about your long-term financial goals now, then you will be in a much better place when it really is time to transition out of the military lifestyle.

TAKING CARE OF TRANSITION BUSINESS

Ideally, you begin the process of transitioning out of the military long before you actually do it (even if only in your mind), and there is a good reason for it.

There is a lot to take care of at the time.

Getting out of the military, you will come to find out, is harder than getting in to it. Add to it the fun of setting up your civilian life and you can see that there is much to do in what inevitably feels like a short time.

While your service member may be the one going through the official military-to-civilian transition, the truth is that the whole family is going through it with him.

It makes sense, doesn't it?

You may not have served in uniform, but you've been a part of this venture since day one.

What needs to happen for your uniformed spouse to become a civilian again? Here's a list for you ponder:

- Your service member will need to call or visit the transition assistance program (TAP) office and sign up for the required training, most recently known as Transition GPS.

Transition Goals, Plans, Success (GPS) is a relatively new redesign of the transition assistance program.

It is made up of four parts:

- preseparation counseling
- five-day workshop (job search skills training)
- career track workshops (accessing higher education, career technical training, and entrepreneurship)
- capstone (final part of Transition GPS where paperwork is signed)

Spouses of transitioning service members are also allowed and encouraged to attend Transition GPS, and you should absolutely plan to go.

- Make sure you completely understand the potential postuniform benefits, entitlements, and periods of eligibility to use them. Some benefits are dated, and if you don't use them in time, you lose them. You also want to know what happens to your existing benefits as this transition is made. For example, what happens to your spouse's Thrift Savings Plan monies? How will you pay for medical expenses going forward? If he's retiring, will you still need an ID card for yourself and the kids?
- Remember when you thought about where you want to live, what want to do, and how much you needed to earn way back when? Now is the time to pull those answers out, dust them off, and update them as necessary.

- Your uniformed spouse should also understand any future employment restrictions that may apply to him or her based on past military experience and security clearance levels. The legal office on the military installation can enlighten him.
- Speaking of security clearance, if your spouse has one, make sure he understands what happens to it after he leaves the military.
- Whoever in the family needs a post-military-life job needs to network for it and begin to actually apply for jobs at about three months from being able to begin work.
- Before you close the door on this chapter of your life, make sure you get copies of your medical and dental records. Schedule appointments now while you aren't paying out of pocket for them.
- If you live on a military installation, contact the housing office for detailed clearing information.
- Visit the finance office to determine what, if any, separation pay you may be entitled to.
- Update your will and power of attorney and/or obtain any free-of-charge-now legal advice through the legal office.
- Line up your transitional health care plan and future insurance benefits.
- If applicable, apply for VA disability benefits.
- Make sure your service member carefully reviews the draft DD 214 worksheet. The final DD 214 will be the proof positive of a military career and will be a necessary document in the years to come for different reasons. Keep the official DD 214 in a safe place. It's a pain to replace if you lose it.
- Hopefully you don't need them, but go ahead and find out about potential unemployment benefits just in case you do.
- Upgrade professional wardrobes.

You can learn more about Transition GPS and the military-to-civilian career transition process at the DoD TAP, www.dodtap.mil. From this page, you can also access each service branch's version of the TAP by clicking on the service branch emblem. Easy.

Retirement is tricky. I wasn't even tracking it, and there it was. Bam!

—Sonia Greer, U.S. Army Spouse

POTENTIAL POSTUNIFORM
BENEFITS AND ENTITLEMENTS

Another important idea to keep in the back of your minds is that there may be important benefits and entitlements available to your separated service member and potentially to you and your family, too.

Examples of such benefits and entitlements include:

- post-9/11 GI Bill benefit transferability
- emergency transition savings account
- Thrift Savings Plan decision
- insurance needs such as life, health, dental, and vision
- moving expenses and cost-of-living considerations
- tax planning
- employer benefit plan costs
- Survivor Benefit Plan elections
- VA disability claim
- separation and/or retirement pay

Examples of VA compensation-related benefits include disability compensation, Dependency and Indemnity Compensation (DIC), and Special Monthly Compensations (SMC).

The VA also provides housing and other insurance benefits to veterans with disabilities, including adapted housing grants, service-disabled veterans insurance, and veterans mortgage life insurance.

TRICARE is also a benefit you may no longer enjoy unless you are retiring. Say hello to high monthly health care payments (assuming your employer offers the option) and be prepared to do a lot of claims paperwork.

If you are retiring, TRICARE morphs into a different version, and you still may find yourself paying more out of pocket.

Your military transition will be able to give you the details you need about these entitlements and benefits when the time comes to make the military-back-to-civilian-life switch. If you just can't wait and want to learn more now, however, here are the resources you can use:

Veterans Benefits Administration, www.benefits.va.gov

I am a Veteran (U.S. Department of Veterans Benefits), www.va.gov/opa/PERSONA/

MILITARY-TO-CIVILIAN CAREER TRANSITION STRATEGIES

When the time does come for you and your spouse to become a civilian family again, you might both find yourselves in the market for new jobs. These tips might help you:

- Market the strengths you acquired as a service member or family member.
- Look for a job that will matter to you.
- Learn the language of the industry you're targeting if you don't already know it.
- Tailor your resume and cover letter to a specific job.
- Network with those who are connected to the job you seek.
- Consider using free military-to-civilian career transition resources.
- Review and revise your LinkedIn profile.
- Follow up your applications and resumes.
- Know how to interview effectively over the telephone or via Skype.
- Be on time for job interviews.
- Be nice to everyone. You don't know who has the power.
- Dress to impress, not distress.
- Send a thank-you note after a job or information interview.
- Don't bring up the subject of money first during a job interview.

Table 8.1. Top Five Military-to-Civilian Free Transition Resources

Bradley-Morris, Inc. (BMI)	http://www.Bradley-Morris.com
CivilianJobs.com	http://www.CivilianJobs.com
Lucas Group	http://www.LucasGroup.com/Military
Orion International	http://www.OrionInternational.com
RecruitMilitary	www.RecruitMilitary.com

I am hopeful for the future yet still working through transition for myself and for our family. And yet I am assured that it will all work out. I will move through the grief and indifference as I have throughout each PCS move and transition in our life. I'm a stronger woman for these experiences, and wouldn't change this journey for that very reason.

—Sonia Greer, U.S. Army Spouse

CONCLUSION

Being a military spouse has been very rewarding. It makes me proud to see my husband in his uniform every day.

—Rebecca Roth, U.S. Air Force Spouse

Military service members and their families are amazing. I might be biased because of my own deep uniformed roots, but I don't think so.

There's a definite reason why less than 1 percent of those in the United States serves our country. Not everyone has the strength, the courage, and the compassion to step up in this world. It takes someone of a certain caliber to be willing to do what others cannot or will not do and to be ready to make the ultimate sacrifice if things come to that.

You don't have to work hard to connect the dots between those who serve in uniform and their families, either.

Extraordinary people attract one another and bring them into the world, too.

A BIT MORE WISDOM FOR THE ROAD AHEAD

Your experience living as a military family will be your own despite the common denominators you may share with others. Embrace it for whatever it ends up meaning to you.

Before you graduate from this basic training, here are few more nuggets of wisdom that don't fit neatly anywhere else in this book, but they belong within its pages nonetheless.

Your extended family. Your family tree is about to grow a few new branches. The names on those twigs do not represent people who are related to you by blood. Rather, they those who are gifted to you compliments of shared military life experiences, for better or worse.

You may even love them more than some of your own biological relatives. You will live next door to them. You will work and play beside them. You will trust them with the care of your children, your pets, and your secrets. You will celebrate promotions, new babies, and graduations with them. You will buy their Pampered Chef and Scentsy products even though you don't need them because you simply want to support them. You will feel their pain when they are hurt and experience their losses. You will cry when you have to move away from them.

If you're lucky, you will find yourself stationed with them again somewhere else down the years. Even if you aren't, it won't matter. Their twigs will grow into strong branches that will stand the test of time.

> Trust your spouse but check the car's backseat for newsletters, holiday party announcements, and mail that he or she might have forgotten to bring in.
>
> —Kristin Sells, U.S. Air Force Brat and U.S. Army Spouse

Life is short. Buy the pottery. Buy the shoes. Drink the wine. Order the dessert. It's more than just a pithy Facebook post; it's excellent advice for any military spouse.

Make the most of your travels as a military family.

If you truly want that set of Polish pottery or whatever materialistic indulgence makes you smile, get it without regret. Experience the culture wherever you are stationed, whether it is Fort Polk, Louisiana, or Tbilisi, Georgia.

One day, when this chapter of your life is far behind you, you'll really be glad you did. Those meaningful keepsakes along with your treasured memories of all your military-life-related adventures will remind you that, for better or worse, you embraced it.

> Always keep a book or deck of cards in your bag. You will almost always wait for appointments. My kids made friends by playing cards at the clinic rather than watching endless hours of TV. The wait is much easier that way.
>
> —Tanya Kerr, U.S. Air Force Spouse (Retired)

Find a good dry cleaning service. Unless you have served in the military yourself, you will never wash, starch, or iron a uniform exactly the way your spouse likes it. It will never be stiff enough or creased in the exact places it should be, and that's okay.

If your spouse won't do it and you clearly can't do it right, find a good dry cleaning service and let them do it. *Every. Single. Place. You. Are. Stationed.*

The expense is more than worth it as it will save you both valuable time and potentially your marriage, too.

> Bloom where you are planted.
>
> —Anonymous Military Spouse

Scratches, dings, and gouges. Every time you move, you will find brand-new scratches, dings, and gouges on your favorite pieces of furniture. The moving paperwork will say so, and you'll put in the requisite claims for damage reimbursement each and every time.

Your heart will also get scratches, dings, and gouges on it throughout your journey as a military family. Don't worry about it, though. Those marks will give both you and your furniture character and remind you of your many adventures in the years to come. Like the wood your dining room table is made of, you are strong, too.

> Stay flexible. Go with the flow. Nothing is ever "for sure," so still plan and be as organized as possible. Enjoy the many experiences and people you'll meet along the way. Remember to support your spouse who is always dealing with many more things and doesn't always have control over situations like timelines, duty hours, and duty stations.
>
> —Anonymous Military Spouse

Loose lips still might sink ships. In March of 2015, the names, photos, and addresses of one hundred U.S. service members were posted online with a call for lone wolf attacks by a hacking division of a known terrorist organization.

Now more than ever before, we need to watch what we say in public or post online so that we don't inadvertently give away information that could draw a target on those we love and on our families.

We don't need to live in fear. Common sense, however, says to think before you say things around others who don't need to hear them, and avoid oversharing the personal details of your life online.

Semper Gumby! Always flexible.

—Kristin M. Sells, U.S. Air Force Brat and U.S. Army Spouse

Keep an address book. Buy an old-fashioned address book and use a pencil to keep it updated. The information will change frequently, and it's much easier than saving it on your computer where files can get deleted. Or, if you don't want the names and addresses of all those contacts ultimately erased and potentially forgotten over time, boldly use a pen and invest in a new address book when the time comes. Turn your old address book into a time capsule.

Each new place has its own unique culture. Give yourself time to learn about it and find where you fit in. Try to be patient with yourself. It will take some time to find your "new normal," but trust that it will happen.

—Jennifer Oswalt, U.S. Air Force Spouse

GRADUATION DAY

Congratulations! You did it.

If you've made it this far in this book, then you can consider yourself graduated. Don't get too excited though. You may know the basics, but there is still much to learn. By this point, you should know that, and you should also know that is okay.

This book, as I mentioned in the introduction, wasn't written to give you all the answers and provide you with all the information you'll ever need. It was, however, designed to give you the basics you need as you stand at or near the start line of your military life.

You'll learn and experience so much more as you move forward in your own good time. You'll learn there are things about this lifestyle you love dearly and wouldn't trade for anything. And to be completely honest, there will be things about it you hate.

For better or worse, military family life is what it is, or *what it isn't*, as my husband likes to say every time I repeat that cliché. Whatever it is, it will be yours and yours alone.

Military Life 101: Basic Training for New Military Families has tried to paint a positive portrait of military life for you, one that is filled with good people having your best interest at heart. The sincerest efforts have been made to include current information and correct information.

Please forgive any important, unintentional omissions in this book. And please remember that information about programs, services, benefits, website addresses, and entitlements change over time and after books have gone to print.

> Embrace the lifestyle. It could be the best or the worst, but it is exactly what you make of it.
>
> —Rebecca Bring, U.S. Air Force Spouse

Like many in the military family, my service branch roots are mixed. My dad and brothers were Marines, my husband a soldier, and my nephew, a soon-to-be newly commissioned officer in the Army after his graduation from college. I've worked closely with families and service members from all branches of the military.

While there may be a healthy professional rivalry between the services on many matters, they can and do come together beautifully when it comes to taking care of our military families.

PARTING WORDS

I was proudly raised as a brainwashed Marine Corps brat, and I later married a hardcore and handsome soldier, so I do have some conflicting service branch feelings on occasion.

For example, when the traditional Army-Navy football game happens I cheer for the Army, and I'm sure my dad, who is guarding the gates of heaven with all the other Marines, thinks me a traitor. Likewise, I hope my Army spouse overlooks my penchant for using a certain Naval expression, one that is often said as a blessing of good fortune to those starting a new chapter in their lives. I think it is fitting for this final moment of your basic training:

Fair winds and following seas.

Janet Farley
March 2016

APPENDIX A: MILITARY LIFE 101 RECOMMENDED READING LIST

Armstrong, Keith, Dr. Suzanne Best, Dr. Paula Domenici, and Bob Dole. *Courage After Fire: Coping Strategies for Troops Returning from Iraq and Afghanistan and Their Families*. Berkeley, CA: Ulysses Press, 2005.

Barnes, Terri. *Spouse Calls: Messages from a Military Life*. St. Paul, MN: Elva Resa Publishing, 2014.

Barnes, Terri, ed. *Stories Around the Table: Laughter, Wisdom and Strength in Military Life*. St. Paul, MN: Elva Resa Publishing, 2014.

Barnett, Brandon W. *A Salute to Our Heroes: The U.S. Marines*. Herndon, VA: Mascot Books, 2010.

Biank, Tanya. *Army Wives: The Unwritten Code of Military Marriage*. New York: St. Martin's Griffin, 2007.

Biden, Jill. *Don't Forget, God Bless Our Troops*. New York: Simon & Schuster/Paula Wiseman Books, 2012.

Brott, Peggie, Alison Buckholtz, et al. *Military Life: Stories and Poems for Children*. St. Paul, MN: Elva Resa Publishing, 2010.

Canfield, Jack, Mark Victor Hansen, and Charles Preston. *Chicken Soup for the Military Wife's Soul*. New York: Backlist, LLC, 2012.

Carter Waddell, Marshele, and Kelly K. Orr. *Wounded Warrior, Wounded Home: Hope and Healing for Families Living with PTSD and TBI*. Grand Rapids, MI: Revell, 2013.

Chapman, Gary D., and Jocelyn Green. *The 5 Love Languages Military Edition: The Secret to Love That Lasts*. Chicago: Northfield Publishing, 2013.

Conetsco, Cherlynn, and Anna Hart. *Service Etiquette*, 5th edition. Annapolis, MD: Naval Institute Press, 2013.

Corbett, Mary. *National Guard 101: A Handbook for Spouses*. El Dorado Hills, CA: Savas Beatie, 2011.

Crooks, Tara, Starlett Henderson, Kathie Hightower, and Holly Scherer. *1001 Things to Love about Military Life*. New York: Center Street, 2011.

Dumler, Elaine Gray. *The Road Home Again: Smoothing the Transition Back from Deployment.* Frankly Speaking, Inc., 2009.

Fallon, Siobhan. *You Know When the Men Are Gone.* New York: NAL, 2011.

Farley, Janet I. *Military-to-Civilian Career Transition Guide,* 2nd edition. Indianapolis: Jist Works, 2009.

Farley, Janet I. *The Military Spouse's Employment Guide: Smart Job Choices for Mobile Lifestyles.* Manassas Park, VA: Impact Publications, 2012.

Farley, Janet I. *Quick Military Transition Guide: Seven Steps to Landing a Civilian Job.* Indianapolis: Jist Works, 2013.

Garrett, Sheryl, and Sue Hoppin. *A Family's Guide to the Military for Dummies.* Hoboken: Wiley, 2008.

Green, Jocelyn. *Faith Deployed: Daily Encouragement for Military Wives.* Chicago: Moody Publishers, 2009.

Green, Jocelyn. *Faith Deployed . . . Again: More Daily Encouragement for Military Wives.* Chicago: Moody Publishers, 2011.

Gross, Mollie. *Confessions of a Military Wife.* El Dorado Hills, CA: Savas Beatie, 2009.

Henderson, Kristin. *While They're at War: The True Story of American Families on the Homefront.* New York: Mariner Books, 2006.

Hightower, Kathie, and Holly Scherer. *Military Spouse Journey.* St Paul, MN: Elva Resa Publishing, 2013.

Kay, Ellie. *Heroes at Home: Help and Hope for America's Military Families.* Bloomington, MN: Bethany House Publishers, 2012.

Kyle, Taya, and Jim DeFelice. *American Wife: A Memoir of Love, War, Faith, and Renewal.* New York: William Morrow, 2015.

Maxwell, Shannon. *Big Boss Brain: Learning About Traumatic Brain Injuries.* Bowie, MD: 4th Division Press, 2010.

Maxwell, Shannon. *Our Daddy Is Invincible!* Bowie, MD: 4th Division Press, 2011.

Moore, David, and Sharon Honeycutt. *R&R: The Ultimate Travel Guide for Military and Veterans: Discounts, Benefits and Tips for Current and Retired Military.* Createspace Independent Platform, 2015.

Pavlicin, Karen M. *Surviving Deployment: A Guide for Military Families.* St. Paul, MN: Elva Resa Publishing, 2003.

Pavlicin-Fragnito, Karen. *Life After Deployment.* St. Paul, MN: Elva Resa Publishing, 2007.

Robertson, Rachel. *Deployment Journal Series for Kids.* St. Paul, MN: Elva Resa Publishing, 2005.

Robertson, Rachel. *Deployment Journal for Spouses.* St. Paul, MN: Elva Resa Publishing, 2008.

Seligman, Melissa. *The Day After He Left for Iraq: A Story of Love, Family, and Reunion.* Skyhorse Publishing, 2008.

Smiley, Sarah. *Dinner with the Smileys.* Brentwood, TN: Hachette Books, 2014.

Sportelli-Rehak, Angela. *Uncle Sam's Kids: Moving Again Mom*. Island Heights, NJ: Abidenme Books Publishing, 2004.

Troutman, Kathryn. *Jobseeker's Guide: Ten Steps to a Federal Job for Military Personnel and Spouses*, 7th edition. Baltimore: Resume Place, 2015.

Vandesteeg, Carol. *When Duty Calls: A Guide to Equip Active Duty, Guard and Reserve Personnel and Their Loved Ones for Military Separations*. Colorado Springs: David C. Cook, 2013.

Vandevoorde, Shellie. *Separated by Duty, United in Love*. New York: Citadel, 2010.

APPENDIX B: COMMON MILITARY TERMS AND EXPRESSIONS

Newbie, be warned. In the beginning, you won't understand everything others are talking about. You may not even understand everything after years of being around the military.

To complicate matters further, each branch of service has its very own language, making cross-communication between the services interesting, to say the least.

The following list is not an exhaustive one by any stretch of the imagination. It is, however, a family-friendly one sans the questionable language that does on occasion appear in military lingo.

Let's just call it the kindergarten word list for new readers, okay? Before you can read, you have to know your letters.

THE PHONETIC ALPHABET

Imagine you're talking to someone in some random military office over the telephone. They ask you to spell your last name for whatever reason, and you begin to do just that. You might hear that person repeat your spelled-out name back to you using the military's version of the alphabet.

Your last name is not Smith.

It is Sierra, Mike, India, Tango, Hotel. And now you know. *Roger that.*

A Alfa	B Bravo
C Charlie	D Delta
E Echo	F Foxtrot
G Golf	H Hotel

I India	J Juliett
K Kilo	L Lima
M Mike	N November
O Oscar	P Papa
Q Quebec	R Romeo
S Sierra	T Tango
U Uniform	V Victor
W Whiskey	X X-Ray
Y Yankee	Z Zulu

GLOSSARY

AA: Assembly area

AAFES: The Army & Air Force Exchange Service or The Exchange

AAM: Army Achievement Medal

AAR: After Action Review. *Honey, I can't come home until I write up this AAR.*

AB: Air base

ACS: Army Community Service

AD: Active duty

AER: Army Emergency Relief or emergency financial assistance

AF: Airfield or Air Force, depending on the context

AFAF: Air Force Assistance Fund

AFAS: Air Force Aid Society

AFB: Air Force Base

AFPC: Air Force Personnel Center

Airdale: Slang for someone in the Air Force. Similar terms: flyboys and zoomies

AOR: Area of responsibility

BAH: Basic Allowance for housing

BAS: Basic allowance for subsistence. This is a monthly food allowance provided to those in the military who do not eat at military dining facilities.

Brats: Military children are brats. This is not a derogatory term. We love our brats.

BSF: Blue Star Families

CAC: Common access card. This allows you to access .mil websites from a government computer.

Cammies. Slang for camouflage uniform

CDC: Child development center
CINC: Commander-in-chief
Civvies: Civilian clothes. Anything that isn't a military uniform.
Coastie: Slang for someone in the Coast Guard
COLA: Cost of Living Allowance
CONUS: Continental United States
Cover: A service member's hat. They have to wear *cover* if they are walking outside.
CPAC: Civilian Personnel Advisory Center
CPO: Civilian Personnel Office
CTO: Commercial Travel Office (also known as SATO, Carlson Wagonlit, Winggate)
DA: Department of the Army
DECA: Defense Commissary Agency
Deck: The floor of a ship or any floor
DEERS: Defense Eligibility Enrollment System
DFAC: Dining facility
DFAS: Defense Finance and Accounting System
DITY: Do it yourself move
DMDC: Defense Manpower Data Center
DOB: Date of birth
DoD: Department of Defense
DoDEA: Department of Defense Education Activity
Dogface: Slang for an army soldier. Similar terms: grunt
DOR: Date of rank
DOS: Date of separation
DPP: Deferred payment plan
DSN: Defense Switched Network or the military telephone system
EFM: Exceptional family member
EFMP: Exceptional Family Member Program
EFT: Electronic funds transfer
EOM: End of month
ETS: Expiration of Term of Service
FAP: Family Advocacy Program
FCC: Family child care
FM: An abbreviation for family member
FSA: Family separation allowance
FTX: Field training exercise
FY: Fiscal year
GAO: Government Accountability Office

Geo-Bach: Geographic bachelor

GS: General schedule (federal employee working in an appropriated fund job)

HHG: Household goods

High and tight: A very short military-style haircut

HOR: Home of record

HQDA: Headquarters, Department of the Army

HRC: U.S. Army Human Resource Command

IA: Individual assignment

IAW: In accordance with

IG: Inspector General

IVMF: Institute for Veterans and Military Families

Jarhead: Slang for a marine. Similar terms: grunts, leathernecks

Last Four: The last four digits of a Social Security number, generally your military sponsor's Social Security number

Leave: Vacation time

Leg: A nonairborne soldier

MCX: Marine Corps Exchange

Medevac: Medical evacuation

MFLC: Military Family Life Counselor or Consultant

MOB: Mobilization

MOS: Military occupation specialty

MP: Military police

MRE: Meals, ready to eat

MTF: Military treatment facility

Mustang: A slang term for an officer in the military who began his or her career as an enlisted service member

MWR: Morale, Welfare, and Recreation

NAF: Nonappropriated Funds

NCO: Noncommissioned Officer

NDAA: National Defense Authorization Act

NEO: Noncombatant Evacuation Operations

NEX: Navy Exchange

NLT: Not later than

NPD: No pay due

o/a: On or about

OCD: Officer of the deck

OCONUS: Outside the Continental United States

OER: Officer evaluation report

OHA: Overseas housing allowance

OP: Observation post

OPSEC: Operational security

OPTEMPO: Operations tempo

Orders: Instructions, communicated either in writing or orally, which tell or command your service member to do something

OSD: Office of the Secretary of Defense

PCS: Permanent Change of Station move

PCS Orders: The official written orders you need in order to begin the arduous process of relocating from one duty station to another.

PERSCOM: U.S. Army Personnel Command or the Human Resources Command

PERSTEMPO: Personnel tempo

POA: Power of attorney

POC: Point of contact

POV: Privately owned vehicle

PPP: Priority placement program

PT: Physical training

PTS: Post-traumatic stress

PTSD: Post-traumatic stress disorder

Qtrs: Quarters or living arrangements

R&R: An abbreviation for rest and relaxation, or time off from a stressful assignment

Reg: Regulation

RIF: Reduction in force

RSVP: Respond if you please

SAC: School-age child

SBA: Small Business Administration

SBP: Survivor Benefit Plan

SCRA: Servicemembers Civil Relief Act

SF: Special Forces

SFL: Soldier for Life

SGLI: Servicemembers Group Life Insurance

SITREP: Situation report (i.e., the status of the current situation)

SLO: School liaison officer

SM: Service member

SOF: Special operations forces

SOP: Standard operating procedure

Space-A: Space available

Squared Away: To have your act together

Squid: Slang for Navy sailor. Similar terms: swabbies and anchor-clankers

SSN/SSAN: Social Security number/Social Security account number
STAP: Spouse Tuition Aid Program
TA: Tuition assistance
TAD: Temporary additional duty
TAP: Transition assistance program
TDY: Temporary duty
TLA: Temporary living allowance
TMO: Transportation management office
TO: Transportation office
TSP: Thrift Savings Plan
UIC: Unit identification code
USO: United Service Organizations
VA: U.S. Department of Veterans Affairs
VSO: Veteran Service Organization
WG: Wage grade
WIC: Women, Infants and Children
YTD: Year to date
Zoomies: Another slang word for someone in the Air Force

MILITARY EXPRESSIONS

ASAP: As soon as possible
At ease: Relax. Take a deep breath.
BLUF: Short for bottom-line up front
Bravo Zulu (BZ): Well done!
Breaking it down Barney style: A very basic explanation that a small child could understand
COB: Close of business.
Copy That: I understand what you said.
[# days] and a wake up . . . : The number of days left before a move or separation from service
Embrace the suck: Deal with it.
Field strip: To take something apart, such as weapon
GI Party: A cleaning party; it is not a real party. If invited, don't go.
Grounded: You're not going anywhere.
Hit the head: Go to the bathroom, which may also be called a *latrine*
Hooah: An enthusiastic Army expression open to interpretation.
[I] got your six: I got your back.
KSS: Short for keep it simple stupid.

Mandatory fun: Usually a "fun" event you have to go whether you want to or not.

Move out. Draw fire: To leave and start doing whatever you going to do

Roger that: I heard what you said. Or simply, yes.

Ruck up: To get ready to go somewhere

Straighten up and fly right: Get your act together

Voluntold: When you are volunteered to volunteer

Zero dark thirty: A time before sunrise. Also expressed as o-dark thirty.

NOTES

INTRODUCTION

1. Karl W. Eikenberry and David M. Kennedy, "Americans and Their Military, Drifting Apart," *New York Times*, May 26, 2013.

2. David Zucchino and David S. Cloud, "U.S. Military and Civilians Are Increasingly Divided," *Los Angeles Times*, May 24, 2015.

CHAPTER 1

1. 2013 Demographics: Profile of the Military Community, pages vi–vii, Executive Summary.

2. 2013 Demographics: Profile of the Military Family Community, pages vi–vii, Executive Summary.

3. 2015 Military Family Lifestyle Survey Executive Summary, Blue Star Families

4. 2014 Military Family Lifestyle Survey Snapshot, Blue Star Families.

CHAPTER 2

1. 2015 Military Compensation and Retirement Modernization Commission Final Report, page 48.

2. Society for Human Resource Management, "2016 Wages Expected to Rise Globally," www.shrm.org/hrdisciplines/compensation/articles/pages/2016 -wages-global.aspx.

3. Tax Exemptions: http://www.dfas.mil/militarymembers/taxinfo/site exemptions.html.

4. Andrew Tilghman, "'Force of the Future': Career Flexibility, Fewer Moves," *Military Times*, September 1, 2015.

5. Leo Shane III, "Obama Signs Defense Bill, Finalizing Military Retirement Overhaul," *Military Times*, http://www.miltiarytimes.com/story/military/pentagon/2015/11/25/obama-ndaa-defense-bill-military-retirement-overhaul/76302160/.

CHAPTER 4

1. Andrew Tilghman, *Military Times*, "PCS Costs Rising across the Force, Even as Moves Decline," September 17, 2015.

CHAPTER 7

1. Dave Philipps, "Study Finds No Link Between Military Suicide Rate and Deployments," *New York Times*, April 1, 2015, http://www.nytimes.com/2015/04/02/us/study-finds-no-link-between-military-suicide-rate-and-deployments.html?_r=0.

2. "Sexual Assault and Sexual Harassment in the U.S. Military, Vol. 2, Estimates for DoD Service Members from the 2014 Rand Military Workplace Study," http://www.rand.org/pubs/research_reports/RR870z2.html.

3. Information about the DoD Safe Helpline taken directly from http://www.rainn.org.

4. US Department of Veterans Affairs, PTSD: National Center for PTSD, http://www.ptsd.va.gov/.

INDEX

ABOUT THE AUTHOR

Janet I. Farley, EdM, is a long-time respected career transition expert within the greater military community. She offers military service members and their families her own brand of compassionate yet straight-forward career management and job search advice via her books and articles. Farley currently writes for the Military Officers Association of America (www .moaa.org) and she is a contributing editor for Military Transition News (www.civilianjobnews.com). She is an employment panel expert for the National Military Spouse Network (www.nationalmilitaryspousenetwork. org) and the author of several other works on career transition, including *The Military Spouse's Employment Guide, The Military-to-Civilian Career Transition Guide,* and *Quick Military Transition Guide.*

THE PEOPLE'S REPUBLIC OF CHINA